HIGH DEFINITION

HIGH DEFINITION

Unforgettable! Vocabulary-Building Strategies Across Genres and Subjects

SARA HOLBROOK

MICHAEL SALINGER

Foreword by Ellin Oliver Keene

Heinemann
Portsmouth, NH

Heinemann
361 Hanover Street
Portsmouth, NH 03801–3912
www.heinemann.com

Offices and agents throughout the world

The authors and publisher wish to thank those who have generously given permission to reprint borrowed material:

"Private Parts" from *The Dog Ate My Homework* by Sara Holbrook. Copyright © 1996 by Sara Holbrook. Published by Wordsong, an imprint of Boyds Mills Press, Inc. Reprinted by permission of the publisher.

"Subtle" from *Am I Naturally This Crazy?* by Sara Holbrook. Copyright © 1996 by Sara Holbrook. Published by Wordsong, an imprint of Boyds Mills Press, Inc. Reprinted by permission of the publisher.

"Novice" and "Reiterate" from *Well-Defined: Vocabulary in Rhyme* by Michael Salinger. Copyright © 2009 by Michael Salinger. Published by Wordsong, an imprint of Boyds Mills Press, Inc. Reprinted by permission of the publisher.

Acknowledgments for borrowed material continue on page 194.

Library of Congress Cataloging-in-Publication Data
Holbrook, Sara.
High definition : unforgettable vocabulary-building strategies across genres and subjects / Sara Holbrook, Michael Salinger ; foreword by Ellin Oliver Keene.
p. cm.
Includes bibliographical references.
ISBN-13: 978-0-325-03149-1
ISBN-10: 0-325-03149-5
1. Vocabulary—Problems, exercises, etc. 2. Vocabulary—Programmed instruction. 3. English language—Roots. I. Salinger, Michael. II. Title.
PE1449.H55 2010
428.1'076—dc22 2010015713

Editor: Harvey Daniels
Production: Elizabeth Valway and Vicki Kasabian
Interior and cover designs: Bernadette Skok
Composition: Cape Cod Compositors, Inc.
Manufacturing: Valerie Cooper

Printed in the United States of America on acid-free paper
14 13 12 11 10 VP 1 2 3 4 5

Contents

FOREWORD by Ellin Oliver Keene vii
ACKNOWLEDGMENTS ix
RESEARCHING WORDS IN THE DIGITAL AGE xi

1 Learning About Words 1

2 Choosing the Words 31

3 High Definition Through **Explanatory Writing** 42
Writing a News Report 44
Writing Business Letters 48
Writing Sequence Descriptions 52
Writing an Obituary 56
Composing an Interview 60

4 High Definition Through **Persuasive Writing** 68
Writing Well-Crafted Argument 73
Developing an Infomercial 75
Writing Editorials and Persuasive Speeches 79

5 High Definition Through **Narrative Writing** 87
Writing a Nonfiction Story 89
Writing Fiction 93
Writing Journal and Diary Entries 96

6 High Definition Through **Descriptive Writing** 106
Writing Character Descriptions 109
Writing Place or Object Descriptions 115
Word Suggestions 120

7 High Definition Through **Writing Poetry** 126
Writing Vocabulary Poems 128
Pattern in Poetry 135
Revision Writing 141

8 High Definition Through **Big Words** 149
The Mentor Text 150
Figurative Language 153

CONCLUSION 164

APPENDICES
A: The Collaboration Cheat Sheet 165
B: Sample News Article for *Cataclysmic* 166
C: Sample Business Letter for *Inept* 167
D: *Miscalculate* Sequence Description 168
E: *Meander* Sequence Description 169
F: Sample Obituary for *Insipid* 170
G: Sample Obituary for *Convivial* 171
H: Sample Interview for *Malevolent* 172
I: Sample Infomercial for *Enthusiasm* 173
J: Sample Op-Ed for *Exclusivity* 174
K: Persuasive Oration for *Helium* 175
L: Sample Political Oratory for *Stealthily* 176
M: Sample Basic Nonfiction Narrative for *Carnivore* 177
N: Sample Basic Fictional Narrative for *Elation* 178
O: Sample Diary Entry for *Nonconformist* 179
P: Character Description for *Flamboyant* 180
Q: Sample Description of a Place for *Extravagant* 181
R: Sample Description of a Thing for *Entanglement* 182
S: Sample Definition Poem for *Subtle* 183
T: Sample Definition Poem for *Redundant* 184
U: Sample Definition Poem for *Novice* 185
V: Sample Definition Poem for *Reiterate* 186
W: Sample Nonfiction Mentor Text for *Prejudice* 187
X: Sample Mentor Text Poems 188
Y: Sample Mentor Text for *Racism* 190

WORKS CITED 191

Foreword

We've long known what *not* to do in vocabulary instruction—looking a word up in the dictionary and writing a sentence revealing the meaning of the word has gone the way of the dodo bird, and good riddance. As teachers, we struggle because we teach words and within a week our students act as if they've never heard of them or fail to incorporate them into their daily usage. Vocabulary is intricately related to overall comprehension, but we seem still to be grasping for answers about how to teach it effectively. Until this book.

Where are the sound vocabulary strategies that oust outdated practices that had led to frustration with student retention and reapplication of words? How can we engage students and share our love of words without making the activities rote or trite? How do we pull kids together to make vocabulary a collaborative learning adventure? How do we make vocabulary instruction an integral part of every week's reading and writing experiences? The new tactics are in this book.

In *High Definition*, Sara Holbrook and Michael Salinger immerse us in a world of what I would call vocabulary *actions*—not activities—actions that promise unprecedented levels of student engagement while learning new vocabulary. From writing obituaries and infomercials to editorials and poems, the authors argue that vocabulary is a full-contact sport and tell stories of students who can't wait to jump in. Students learn words inside out and go beyond writing about them—though the writing actions have great depth and interest—to performance actions. Sara and Michael describe the actions in such a way that we feel as if we're right there watching words take on a life of their own.

Choosing words for vocabulary instruction is a particular challenge for teachers. Not only do Sara and Michael devote a chapter to choosing words, they provide numerous lists of words at different levels should teachers have the luxury of choosing their own words. They make the case to cull vocabulary words from multiple sources: their own lists, words from students' content-area study, and words that kids discover in their own reading and content-area study.

Sara and Michael believe that vocabulary is a highly collaborative adventure for kids and provide the research to show that they stand on solid ground. From their Collaboration Cheat Sheet to a huge range of tactics suggested to immerse kids in collaborative work, they show how teachers can shift the responsibility to students working in groups to uncover the nuances of words. It is this type of collaborative work that will make the vocabulary words they experience memorable.

This is not a book written merely by two authors who enjoy each other's company and professional interests. Michael and Sara are a married couple whose professional journeys have taken them from the corporate world through nonprofit work into teaching. These broad perspectives inform and enlighten this book with numerous examples of the ways words come to life in contexts outside of school. The embedded banter between these two very funny people makes the reading fly by and is unlike anything I've ever seen in a professional book. I was tempted to skip ahead to the next conversation between Michael and Sara in rather the same way that you skip through the *New Yorker* magazine looking for the comics!

Reading this book is pure pleasure because one senses that these are authors who really know, really enjoy kids. Springing from the pages is their sense of joy in watching kids who take learning into their hands. Sara and Michael laugh with students and teachers and stand back in awe at their insights. If you didn't know how skilled and successful these authors were, you'd get the feeling that every day they're in classrooms is their first day of teaching filled with the wonder of kids.

High Definition is bound to be an important resource for teachers who want to add a dynamic new angle to vocabulary learning. It's also a book for teachers who want workable, research-backed teaching tactics that transform rote vocabulary learning into a vibrant, living, breathing component of each day's literacy block. Though teachers are the conduit, mostly this book is for kids who have not yet discovered the beauty of and fascination with words. This is their ticket into an utterly different kind of vocabulary learning—an energy-juiced, falling in love with words. I wish I were back in school again, and my teacher had read this book.

—Ellin Oliver Keene

Acknowledgments

We are very grateful to several teachers for opening their classrooms to us, including Libby Royko (grade 8), Eastlake Middle School, Eastlake, Ohio; Teena Mitchell (grade 4), Charles Lake Elementary, Cleveland, Ohio; Donna Kohn (grade 10), Mentor High School, Mentor, Ohio; Carol Reinhardt (grade 12), Walnut Creek High School, Des Moines, Iowa; Renee Voce (grade 3), Emerick Elementary, Purcellville, Virginia; Christine Landaker-Charbonneau (grade 8) and Kelli Prodanas (special ed), Pierce Middle School, Milton, Massachusetts.

It was at Bay Village Middle School in Bay Village, Ohio, where we did the bulk of our work with vocabulary writing and performance learning. Thank you to principal Sean Andrews for his continued support. Sixth-grade veteran teacher Katie Lufkin (language arts/social studies) has provided continuing advice and direction identifying the classroom needs of student writers and teachers throughout the writing of this book. To her we extend special thanks. She was also instrumental in introducing us to content-area classrooms where we teamed with science teachers Laurel Beck and Brent Illenberger, social studies teachers Robbie Tupa and Angela Randjelovic, math teacher Mark Kevesdy, and language arts/social studies teacher Sherri Deal to demonstrate definition writing and performance with everything from integers and random patterns to the feudal system and human reproduction.

Sara: We learned a lot from those lessons.

Michael: I already knew about the reproduction system.

Researching Words in the Digital Age

Remember when "look it up" meant going to the corner of the classroom where the unabridged dictionary, the size of a picnic ice chest, was precariously perched on a podium—two-thousand-plus pages of pure intimidation waiting to pin you under its mass? Then, once you had slogged your way through the tome, the definition left you no less baffled?

Times sure have changed. In this book, we invite students to explore, research, and play with words, using both print and digital sources to build their understanding. Here are some sources we rely on:

- **Google.com:** Google! So ubiquitous that it is now a verb—but, add the term *define:* (don't forget the colon) and its vocabulary-building superpower is unleashed; i.e., ***define: reflection*** returns everything from *mirror* to the name of a German thrash metal band along with related phrases. Plus you have the added benefit of spell-check. Click on the images link for a visual representation (if this option is not blocked at school).
- **Dictionary.com** supplies definitions from multiple sources with a single query. A list of antonyms, related topics, and words commonly confused with your term pop up right beside your search. Word origin, as well as medical, science, and cultural dictionaries, are also presented. Plus, an elegant woman pronounces the word at a mouse click. The site tweets daily, and has a Facebook presence and a cool iPhone app.
- **Wordcentral.com:** Merriam-Webster's student-centered online offering includes vocabulary-building games, a thesaurus, rhyming

dictionary, pronunciation, and provides suggestions for words that may have multiple meanings.

- **Wordsmyth.net** provides definitions at three levels: *Beginners, Children's,* and *Advanced* as well as synonyms, antonyms, and audio pronunciations. *The Word Explorer* link leads to related terms.
- **Kids.yahoo.com/reference** is the online kids' version of the *American Heritage Dictionary*. Submit a word and receive pronunciations, multiple definitions, and etymologies, plus a direct link to an encyclopedia and relevant articles.

Welcome to word study, digitized and supercharged. No need to know exactly how to spell the word, just be close enough and a cartoon hallway of doors open to spark inquiry and ignite peer discussion. And welcome to *High Definition*.

Learning About Words

Learning Words

"What's a flame?"

Ben was standing on the beach with his marshmallow on a stick when he was given the directive to "hold it over the flame." After three whole years on the planet, Ben knew the word *fire* and he certainly understood the concept of *hot*, but ***flame*** was a new one. He hesitated.

"A flame is the fire, those little ribbons coming up."

Ben nodded and proceeded to lower his bobbling stick over the flame.

"Flame," he grinned, and the assembled picnickers gave him a collective "atta-boy."

The way Ben learned the word *flame* was ideal. Compared to being given a list of unfamiliar words and definitions on Monday, putting those words into sentences, and being tested on Friday (the least effective way to acquire vocabulary), this method was not only more palatable, but also more effective. He had an authentic reason to want to learn the word, he immediately put the word into action, and, finally, he got a reward for learning the new word in the form of a toasty treat and some adult acknowledgment.

So, what's the message here? We need to light a fire under the vocabulary lessons, pass out treats? Help students acquire enough vocabulary skills so that they don't spend their lives on an isolated beach somewhere, their uncooked metaphorical marshmallows on a stick, not knowing where to put them? Actually, there are so many lessons buried in that little story it's hard to know where to start.

> ***Michael:*** Let's start by observing that the young man was actively involved in his own learning. He was curious and self-motivated to learn about the word *flame*.
>
> ***Sara:*** In this case he became involved immediately through stick-in-hand learning, you might say.
>
> ***Michael:*** Involvement can also mean discussion, collaborative writing, and performance.

Getting and keeping kids involved in growing vocabularies with lifetime benefits is what this book is about. Free use of exciting new vocabulary words cannot be achieved with the old paradigm of the student working in isolation to define and use words in a written sentence. It is through interaction and the conversations that sprout from these exchanges of ideas that curiosity is aroused and genuine and lasting understanding is engendered.

Figure 1.1 *Sixth-Grade Peer Discussion*

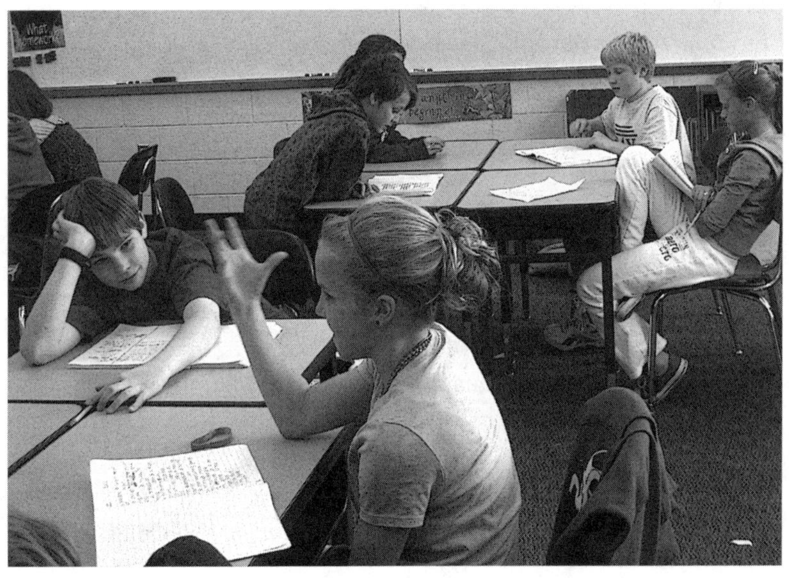

Kids are best motivated to learn when they are both curious and see an authentic reason to develop knowledge of new concepts. Whether those concepts emerge from assigned literature, a science unit on reproduction, or a social studies lesson on the feudal system, teaching really means getting students connected. And what engages middle school students? Their peers do, plain and simple. Ask a class the meaning of ***ubiquitous*** and you often get cold stares. Let them inquire of each other who is ahead in *Dancing with the Stars* or what tanked yesterday's football game and the conversation explodes. For this reason, we have built extensive student interaction into our word-learning strategy.

Do students learn new words from encountering them in their reading? Sure, but according to Nagy, "only about 25–50% of annual vocabulary growth can be attributed to incidental learning from context while reading" (Nagy, Herman, and Anderson 1985). In order to teach a deeper understanding of a broader array of words, vigorous classroom strategies for teaching word knowledge are needed.

Discovering what doesn't work is a snap. Been there, done that; the vast majority of us have had it inflicted upon us. What *does* work is building connections among students as well as between words. In our lessons we follow a sequence of activities leading to student comprehension (see Figure 1.2).

How This Book Works

In this book you will see how we have taught vocabulary in grades 4 through 10 by engaging students in various writing genres. Nothing tricky or esoteric here; these are all writing genres taught in the classroom: explanatory, persuasive, narrative, descriptive, and poetry. Each lesson provides teachers with opportunities to teach and reteach various writing genres while embedding new vocabulary words. We have provided some word lists as a starting point, but naturally you will want to pull in words from your classroom's units of study. (See Chapter 2, "Choosing the Words.")

We have provided samples for each genre that can be copied and projected to provide a basis for instructional discussion before each writing assignment. (See the appendices.) Within the chapters we have included student samples to show how kids have been able to increase their understanding of new vocabulary words by incorporating collaboration, writing, and performance.

Figure 1.2 *Student Comprehension Chart*

Well-Chosen Words **+**	• students have a voice in choosing the words • words come from and are applicable to their own lives • words are related to classroom units of study
Collaborative Discussion **+**	• students research deeper word meaning with and through peer discussion • discussion leads to real-world applications • interaction provides positive social setting and builds a community of learners
Genre Writing **+**	• students embed the words in stories, letters, poems of their own creation • students are able to practice genre writing while learning new words • writing in pairs and small groups enables more discussion throughout the writing process
Performance Learning **=** ***A Growing Vocabulary***	• performance inspires kids to write and revise • affords additional opportunity for peer discussion • provides teachers with added opportunity to reteach the new word

There's one tool that we use consistently with students in the classroom and throughout this book: we call it the Collaboration Cheat Sheet. It looks like this:

The Collaboration Cheat Sheet

Word ______________________________

is can does	**Version 1**
is not cannot does not won't	

The Cheat Sheet is a place where students can capture all their thinking, talking, and writing about a word they are studying. On the left-hand side, kids jot down everything they discover about the word, including what it is (synonyms) and what it is not (antonyms). As these notes accumulate, the Cheat Sheet then becomes a prewriting tool, as kids turn to creating a text in any genre. The right-hand side of the form leaves room for a rough draft of the students' writing. A second, more polished version, if relevant, can be written below the first if there's room or on another piece of paper. You may duplicate the Cheat Sheet in Appendix A or project the

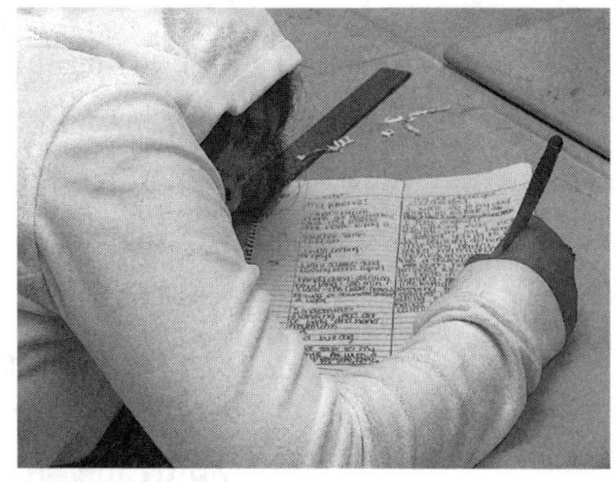

Figure 1.3 *Ninth-Grade Student Writes*

Perilous version one

is	
dangerous	I am perilous
revolving doors	I am the danger
injury	That can be lurking
~~[illegible]~~	In revolving doors and
fireworks	fireworks
pain	I am perilous
	I am not safe or non harming
	I can cause injury
	I am not there to protect.
	I am perilous
not	Version two
safe	I am perilous
non harmful	the danger that may
	be lurking in revolving doors
	and fireworks
	I am perilous
	not safe or non harming
	Injuries can be caused
	I am not there to protect
	For I,
	Am perilous

Figure 1.4 *Collaboration Cheat Sheet in Action with Eighth-Grade Vocabulary Word:* **Perilous**

model and have students fold their papers in half lengthwise to make their own. This simple structure helps students think beyond economical dictionary definitions and clarifies any confusing thesaurus connections. Students will begin to look for real-world examples of words—how they work, what they're capable of, and where they might logically be used—imprinting a deeper understanding of meaning on kids and ensuring better use in the future.

Well-Chosen Words

This is where we would hope to tell you *the* best way to choose vocabulary words for independent instruction. Problem is, there isn't one. We partnered with teachers in literature and content-area classrooms and will discuss their varied approaches to selecting vocabulary words in Chapter 2, "Choosing the Words." As you will read, each teacher took a different approach. In each instance, when we were working in the classroom, we encouraged the students to take a role in selecting which words we would examine for further study as a means of engaging them in the lessons.

In *Bringing Words to Life: Robust Vocabulary Instruction*, Isabel Beck and her colleagues cite their own personal, lifelong infatuations with words and preface their book with an admonition to "[provide] rich information about words, frequent opportunities to use and consider the words, and extending attention to words beyond the vocabulary lesson" (Beck, McKeown, and Kucan 2002).

Wouldn't it would be fabulous if all of our students came to us with this same infatuation for words? Alas and alack. Not always true. Some students don't want to be accused of learning how to "talk smart"; that is, talking in a way that is seen to betray their culture as a result of a notion that if someone is book smart, he or she can't be street smart, and vice versa. This idea is as prevalent as it is misguided. Teachers not only have to introduce rivers of new terminology to kids, but they need to find ways to inspire the often reluctant learners who are more accustomed to the speed of text talk and cordoned by peer pressure to take the time to understand new words. How do we inspire our students to harness the power of unfamiliar words into effective communication?

Sara: Reluctant is almost too weak a word to describe middle school kids' responses to new vocabulary.

Michael: How about ***loath***, then?

Loath is a strong word. But any teacher who has challenged a sunny day with the phrase *vocabulary lesson* only to see a dark cloud descend over the room knows that students can be downright word resistant.

Michael: Antagonistic?

Sara: Averse?

No matter the label you choose, the sentiment seems to be universal: Vocabulary lessons are too often a dreaded downer, a gloomy fun house passageway where students and teachers alike are often blindly feeling their way along; the result being not so much fun at all.

Many teachers combine direct vocabulary instruction in language arts along with the reading of a text—a novel, short story, or poem—teaching new words in context. Teacher support is essential with this approach since research tells us students will be able to understand a new word strictly from written context clues only about 5 to 15 percent of the time (Nagy, Herman, and Anderson 1985).

Sometimes, trying to learn a new word in the context of its dictionary definition is even more confusing. Take the definition of ***cardinal***. That can either be a number, a bird, or a priest in a red hat. Some human interaction in the form of discussion is required to know which definition is right in which context. Look up ***jubilant*** in the Merriam-Webster online dictionary and you get a one-word definition: ***exultant***. Not much use to your average sixth grader.

Comedian David Steinberg offers a classic routine about being a student and responding to an essay question while not understanding the vocabulary and at a loss for context clues: "Refute the allegation that the literature of the Middle Ages was ***moribund***." Steinberg responds first with wide eyes and then, as if writing: "Some believe that the literature of the Middle Ages was moribund. Some believe that the literature of the Middle Ages was not moribund. I believe that the literature of the Middle Ages was not moribund. In order to refute the allegation that the literature of the Middle Ages was moribund, one would need to have a detailed knowledge of the literature and history of that period," (*Whispering to self*) "which I wish to God I had." His response (while hilariously familiar) reads like a student distress call for direct vocabulary instruction. In fact, if Student Steinberg had known the meaning of the word *moribund* he probably could have been able to answer this question. In fact, he was able to successfully use *moribund* in a sentence, but clearly he did not understand the word's meaning.

> ***Michael:*** We like to start a vocabulary lesson with students by asking them to humor us with some word association.
>
> ***Sara:*** We say *hot dog*, they say *mustard*.
>
> ***Michael:*** We say *ice cream*, they say *yummy*.
>
> ***Sara:*** We say *vocabulary lesson—*
>
> ***Michael:*** They say BORING.
>
> ***Sara:*** Once I had a student say, "I'm outta here."

No matter what words they choose, the sentiment is the same. Vocabulary lessons too often fall somewhere between a splinter and a root canal on the pleasure index. And this response is not limited to students, either. We've played this word association game with groups of teachers and heard a similar collective groan in response to the phrase *vocabulary lesson*.

Sandra Whitaker says, "Children need thorough, lively vocabulary instruction to learn the sheer joy of language," noting that "when word study isn't playful it becomes dry quickly and students lose interest" (2008).

> ***Sara:*** So let's collectively acknowledge that for kids to keep growing their vocabularies, we need to be actively identifying words for further study (with the help of our students).
>
> ***Michael:*** Varied and extensive research tells us this is true. So then we need to seek out and adopt classroom strategies to make this happen in fun, interesting ways.
>
> ***Sara:*** We can't simply rely on them to learn all words that they need to know through their reading.

What we have not included in this book is an official, leveled word list. Our aim is to suggest ways that you and your students can help identify words that matter, words that they want and need to know right now, robust words they believe are worth taking the time to actually learn. So, with the understanding that there is no single right way to choose the words, for the purposes of this book we *have* included a word list with every lesson that you may wish to use to model the writing exercises.

Collaborative Discussion

After we have selected the words, how do we teach the words?

> ***Sara:*** Let's talk about it.
>
> ***Michael:*** And then let's talk some more.
>
> ***Sara:*** And then let's have the kids talk.

Anyone who has ever uttered the words, "Class, take out a piece of paper," knows that kids talk. Steering that propensity for conversation

Figure 1.5 *Eighth graders smile through a vocabulary discussion.*

toward acquiring new words is one step toward collaborative learning. In the course of their discussions, kids surround new words with vocabulary and concepts that are familiar to them, helping them to see how that word works in their own worlds. When kids discuss new words, talking about their meanings, the conversation furthers their deeper understanding of those words and concepts, all the while keeping them engaged.

Collaborative learning is more than just talk. *Just talk* is what kids engage in all the time, conversing with peers, mimicking television and other media presentations that have been engineered to be easily comprehensible. Collaborative learning is active learning.

We want them to grow beyond everyday slang, to reach for more precise language. Capitalizing on students' propensity for talk by building a collaboration step into every lesson, we've found student success in understanding new words through peer support. In other words, most of our students' daily communication is with those who speak their language, albeit limited. It is mostly in the classroom where students are encouraged to stretch the boundaries of the familiar, utilizing new words. However, as you have undoubtedly seen, even in a school setting language can be limited by peer pressure. Substituting peer support for peer pressure leads to learning with kids.

When we began this project, our initial game plan was to introduce a writing genre to students (letter, story, poem), provide them with dictionary resources, some new words, and let them have at it—writing to learn. But what we witnessed was that while working in small groups, prewriting discussion became a major learning component. In fact, it was in the collaboration before the writing began that much of the learning took place. For us, this really redefined the term ***prewrite*** to mean an oral exchange of ideas.

When students read on their own, an unfamiliar word is a stopper. As we watched students working in collaboration with others in pairs and small groups, we saw how encountering a new word becomes a discussion starter. It turns out that working in isolation is not nearly as useful in helping kids reach for clarity in language as a good argument over the meaning of a word is, since discussion requires students to think about the word.

Sara: I had a professor, Lyle Crist, who used to continually remind us that "all writings are afterthoughts."

Michael: One can hope.

Sara: So what better inspiration than the oral exchange of thoughts?

Talking before writing about words is thinking aloud, relating those words to stories and images. Connecting words with images is what helps students learn from the earliest ages. Classroom writing guide Donald Graves reminds us, "When children 'invent' spelling, they demonstrate one of the best examples of applied learning for sound/symbol relationships" (1990). A word is nothing more than a representative symbol. ***House*** is not simply h-o-u-s-e; the individual letters or sounds attached to them carry no meaning. The word as a whole is a symbol for a structure, a living place. Therefore, participating in the invention of scenes to illustrate proper word use improves the word/symbol relationship and provides evidence of applied learning. A word is just a collection of letters until it is connected in the student's mind with an image; here the sum truly is greater than the whole. Through conferring with peers, a word passes from simple phonemic decoding and into understanding as it is synthesized on a conceptual level.

Michael: I'd be willing to go out on a limb here and state that all written words are representative of an image.

Sara: We saw this in the hieroglyphics during our tour through the ruins in Egypt.

Michael: Don't forget the petroglyphs in the mountains outside of Phoenix.

Sara: A couple billion Asians manage written communication through image-evoking symbols.

Michael: So, even though the individual letters may represent sounds—once they are assembled into a word—ta-da, it's a picture!

Graves further recommends that a classroom be "decentralized" in order to facilitate learning. "When the classroom is decentralized and highly structured, children can help each other, thus providing maximum opportunity for both teacher and learning about word and meaning problems" (1990, 77). The focus needs to radiate out from the teacher, involving all of the students actively in the learning process.

Last year at the Thanksgiving table we heard about an assignment that Michael's seventh-grade niece Emma had recently struggled to complete. After reading *The Giver*, Emma's teacher had assigned the following: students were each to write and lay out a newspaper. The teacher provided a list of fifteen themes in the novel (individuality, euthanasia, multigenerational families, diversity, etc.). Each student, on her own, was to identify three of these themes and for each theme compose an article or op-ed, find an article in a real newspaper on that theme and change the names of the principals to match the characters in the novel, and create a word jumble or advertisement (something besides an article that can be found in a newspaper). This is a huge task—multiplied by three—with no audience for the students' work besides the teacher. Emma, as did all the other students, had to work on her own. Emma, who had recently read *Jane Eyre* for fun, is in honors English, and is rarely seen without a book in her hands. Yet she was maintaining a B– in reading because of her struggle to complete the writing portion and the layout challenges (it all had to fit, typed, on one large sheet of paper) for this solo assignment. When her mother questioned the assignment, the teacher expressed her own frustration, bemoaning the fact that "many of the students didn't even bother to turn the assignment in."

What could have been a fun, collaborative, learning classroom activity among the students had been turned into a frustrating kitchen-table collaboration with Mom. Within the family, we have taken to calling this story Emma's Dilemma. Educator Kelly Gallagher might put it slightly differently and say that Emma was served a heaping portion of his "Kill-a-Reader Casserole." In his book *Readicide*, he observes that too often classroom strategies "subject [students] repeatedly to treatments that are counterproductive to developing book lovers" (Gallagher 2009). How much more fun and helpful to Emma had she been invited to dish about *The Giver* with peers and collaborate in a culminating activity.

Learning groups become even more essential when we talk about the extraordinary task of mastering new words. After all, the ability to use words to communicate with one another is what distinguishes us humans. To advocate that the best way to learn new words is on our own, reading and writing in isolation, just seems counterproductive.

> Groups can raise individuals' levels of aspirations. Groups can inspire individuals to achieve beyond their wildest expectations. Groups can give individuals insights and understandings that could never be achieved alone. Groups can ferment creativity and the unlocking of potential. Groups can change the way people perceive the world and the reality of their lives. Groups can provide variety and entertainment, and fun. If students were required to work alone all day, classroom life could be lonely, dull, boring and alienating. (Johnson and Johnson 2004)

Dull and alienating is no way to excite kids about reading, writing, or new vocabulary, that's for certain. Our belief is that performance and working in small groups will help the resistant learner. Starting with smaller work groups will encourage greater participation among the students and provide a springboard toward the ultimate goal of that front of the classroom presentation. Kids are pack animals by nature; we should use this sociology to our benefit.

Sara: As the poet formerly known as a business writer, I am mystified by the amount of stress we place on our lessons and our students, insisting that they write autonomously. As if creative thinking is strictly a solo activity. It's not.

Michael: What amazes me is how much collaboration goes into books about how to teach kids to write autonomously. It seems *et al.* is a ubiquitous contributing author to these tomes. In fact, bouncing thoughts off each other makes ideas grow and morph into new ideas.

Sara: Exactly. Why aren't more of our student research papers, speeches, letters, essays, and even stories written through collaboration? They are in the working world.

Michael: "We Get By with a Little Help from Our Friends"—a Lennon and McCartney collaboration written for their friend Ringo.

Great thinkers such as Paz and Berry, great educational researchers such as Johnson, Daniels, Nagy, Allen, Gallagher, and Harvey, and great inventors such as Walt Disney and Bill Gates—heck, even an award-winning quarterback crediting his linemen—all of them know that people succeed most often as part of a team. If we design our writing lessons as if our goal were to train future reclusive novelists heading for a life in a closeted garret, we not only make kids miserable, we are missing out on leading them to discover practical, real-world thinking and communication skills.

Michael: The Unabomber was a solo writer.

Sara: I'm not sure the cause and effect works on that one.

The alternative to real-world collaborative writing is the solo artist, working in isolation and creating art for art's sake—a goal that poet/philosopher/farmer Wendell Berry considers "adolescent thinking" perpetuated by critics whose main purpose has been to nurture a "rich commerce in subsidies, grants, and teaching jobs" (Berry 1983). Berry observes, "Nothing human exists without a human purpose somewhere back of it and a human effect somewhere ahead of it. If things are made to serve no good purpose, then they corrupt their causes, and they have bad effects."

Michael: Careful. Start quoting poets and philosophers and we risk diminishing the perceived practicality of this book.

Sara: Yes, but sometimes, don't you worry that this academic thinking has trickled down to the desks of kids with exactly what Berry calls "bad effects," kids made miserable by being forced into writing as a solo activity and then workshopping pieces into mush after the fact conferring with just their teachers? We need to frontload the workshop process, allowing kids to think aloud, talking to one another before, during, and after committing words to paper.

Michael: We need to teach writing in a way that helps kids become thinkers. Not blood-on-the-forehead, pencil-chewing strugglers, but dynamic thinkers. It's too easy for a teacher to look at a student's writing and make suggestions to improve what is on the page and think the job is done.

Sara: Right, we call this fixing the writing rather than helping the writer—even the best-intentioned instructors can make this slipup. We have found it more beneficial for our students to help one another along the way.

Michael: Our job as instructors is to create a climate in which rigorous discussion and deeper thinking is valued among peers.

Sara: Assuming all things human have an effect, we can't be satisfied with a neat grade or a satisfactory test score as the only measure of our instruction's effectiveness.

Words, Berry goes on to say, are never autonomous. Each word is "married," and creates a "connection between words and speakers, words and acts, words and things" (1983, 31). Allowing students to talk through these connections through collaboration before, during, and after writing will help them become better thinkers, which we both believe to be the best outcome for our teaching.

Through well-chosen words, collaborative discussion, and extra-double-duty practice in their genre writing, students benefit from being actively involved in their own language development. Sharing their learning, actually saying the words aloud and talking about them, is the last step in helping to fix word meanings in students' minds.

Outdated theories about learning vocabulary in isolation, hunched over a worksheet, assumes that language is fixed, like a mathematical equation, when in fact language and word meaning are in a constant state of flux. A quick visit to urbandictionary.com provides unlimited examples.

> ***Michael:*** Did you hear President Obama recently accusing the media of getting *wee-wee'd* up over irrelevant issues? That was a new one to me.
>
> ***Sara:*** Yeah. I always thought *wee wee* was something you did behind the closed bathroom door, not on the TV in front of grandma and everyone.

"Fixity is always momentary," says Mexican poet/philosopher and Nobel Prize–winner Octavio Paz. "Man does not speak because he thinks; he thinks because he speaks. Or rather, speaking is no different than thinking: to speak is to think." In his writings on language, he goes on to point out that we are constantly "re-establishing meanings" as we think and talk, concluding that "community does not formulate language, language forms community" (1990). Thinking leads to understanding. What is conversation and collaboration if not thinking aloud?

Because language is used for communication between humans and because of its dynamic nature, collaborative discussion is a crucial ingredient in our formula for vigorous vocabulary instruction. But we don't stop there. We like to keep students engaged in collaboration right through the writing process and into a culminating performance.

Genre Writing

Most of us have seen that list of vocabulary words looming on the classroom's black-, white-, or smart board, piled like bricks daring students to try and bust through. Whether you call it a word wall, this week's vocabulary, or building blocks to a better lexicon, these floating stacks of words still need to be surmounted—or better yet, disassembled into manageable bits and passed around.

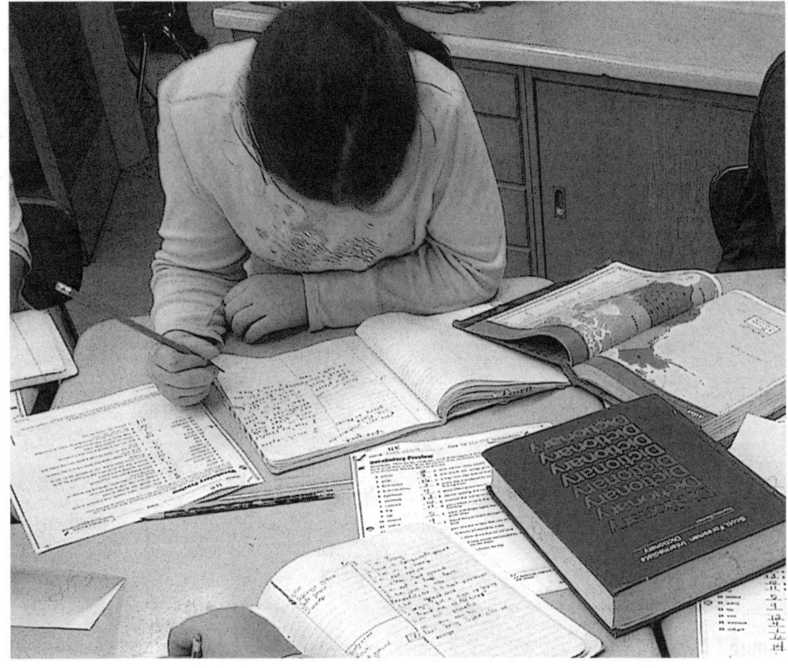

Figure 1.6 *A fifth grader treks through new social studies vocabulary.*

> ***Michael:*** Alongside those classrooms' "word walls" are often posted tips for improving writing in a variety of genres.
>
> ***Sara:*** Tips for a good business letter, elements of a strong paragraph, instructions reminding writers to use active verbs, obviously important because they have all kinds of charts and bulleted lists.
>
> ***Michael:*** We know that teachers have to refer back to them repeatedly. *They're laminated.*
>
> ***Sara:*** Teaching the components of good writing is not simply a lesson; it's an ongoing process.

That's our goal here—to take the writing lessons, which are already included in the curriculum and which require repeated instruction, and load them up like a twice-baked potato with bacon bits, to fold vocabulary lessons into explanatory, narrative, persuasive, and creative writing assignments like raisins into an oatmeal cookie. In this way our students learn and internalize new words, making them an authentic part of a finished written product.

This type of vocabulary instruction is looking at a word not as an assemblage of letters, but more like a story. Maybe the word is the

Torrid: Intense heat

is: hot, extreme heat.

can: Sweat, fire, Sun, boiling, burn, Summer equator, melt, desert, volcano

is not: cool, Cold, ice, Snow, Winter

Cant: Chill, freeze, Solid

doesn't like: freezer, pools, rain

To be torrid would feel as though you are stuck in a volcano.
A constant unpleasing Sweat, that is never relieved.
When it Snows it makes rain and when it freezes comes melting.
I feel as though I'm wearing a Sweater on the Sun.
To be hot is an understatement, I boil I burn I scorch and I flame.
Nothing is cold or ice as a matter of fact what is ice?
The equator is much too cold for me.
Just throw me in the fire So I may burn, I am much too torrid for you on earth.

Figure 1.7 *A* **Torrid** *Descriptive Paragraph by Eighth Grader, Kari*

protagonist, or the setting, or the antagonist. A word might be the motivation, the excuse, or the apology. Based on this concept, we've taken all of our best ideas from our poetry-writing lessons, leaning heavily on our poetic companions of *personification* and *figurative language*, and used them as a catalyst for a variety of writing genres to formulate some fun, memorable, and unique recipes for vocabulary acquisition for your students. Finally, we advocate that you have those students serve them up to their peers through oral presentation.

Michael: For a second there I thought we were working on a cookbook.

Sara: Well, mixing metaphors at the very least. Hazards of having two cooks in the kitchen, I guess.

Michael: Although writing in a pair or small group does offer learning benefits, such as the opportunity to discuss word meanings as part of the prewrite.

We began to look at the value of enriching and expanding student vocabulary by engaging them in writing definition poems. That exercise worked so well we decided to expand the idea, framing new words in a variety of forms of writing. Poetry is a great tool for learning, but as poets we also are forced to admit that there are other text types and skills that are rightfully required in a well-rounded curriculum, including explanatory, persuasive, narrative, and descriptive writing.

In this book we branch out from poetry into a slew of complementary genres for our vocabulary-writing lessons, going beyond (but not abandoning) poems. We do kick to the curb the much tried, but rarely successful, "Put the word in a sentence."

Michael: I've always been a proponent of multitasking—eating and driving, running on a treadmill while reading or watching a movie, taking the dog into the shower with me . . .

Figure 1.8 *Sixth graders perform vocabulary lessons in science class.*

Sara: I would say that I can drive, eat my breakfast, put on makeup, and talk on the phone at the same time, but I think that's illegal even with a hands-free device. How about I just say I like to talk on the phone while loading the dishwasher?

Enter classroom performance, stage right.

Performance Learning

In this book we use a multifaceted, communal approach to keep our vocabulary lessons fun and lively while remaining instructive. First, we encourage peer collaboration about the words, and then have students implant the vocabulary lesson in a writing exercise, and, finally, add a sociable performance-learning component to every lesson. Performance becomes a way to reuse the words in a playful and memorable way, share the learning with others, and serve as an assessment tool.

A group of words whose only reason for existence is their possibility of inclusion on some standardized test months down the road is not going to evoke the same level of curiosity from a student as the one he or she has discovered through personal investigation. Motivation to learn is more likely to materialize if the pupil sees an immediate use for the word. By building in a performance component to our lessons, students will recognize a need to completely understand a word's meaning. We all work harder if a goal is in sight. Throughout this text you will see us pairing vocabulary-writing exercises with one form or another of performance. Along with the fun factor associated with classroom presentations, we believe that pairing lessons with performance enhances and ingrains instruction.

Combining motor movements with learning helps students internalize new information. Kinesthetic memory has been lauded by experts as disparate as educator Susan Griss (1998). "Interpreting a concept through physical means helps [students] to grasp, internalize, and maintain abstract information," and that malaprop maestro Yogi Berra, who once quipped, "Think? How can you hit and think at the same time?" (Beilock 2007). In other words, once we have married our thinking to a physical activity, the learning becomes internalized.

Michael: I always think of the teacher who told me that the only Spanish verbs she remembers from her high school classes are the three that she and a partner acted out in front the class.

Sara: Tell kids that they will have to present their work aloud to the class and at first they will protest. Vehemently. And then they quickly turn back to the writing to polish it. They talk it over with whomever is next to them, questioning, "Does this make sense?"

Presenting their vocabulary work in front of an audience requires students to think about the word and provides them with an authentic reason to use the new word in context. Of course, the listeners also benefit because they are then able to pair a new word with a visual image.

Sara: I'm thinking about the middle school scholar who acted out his piece of writing about the word ***constipated***.

Michael: Strong image-to-word connection?

Sara: Truly unforgettable.

Michael: I like to have kids act out my poem "Lugubrious." One student personifies the antonym by laughing and smiling while the ***lugubrious*** one falls down on the floor wailing and crying (Salinger 2009).

Sara: No one does drama better than a middle schooler.

Dramatic is memorable and student performance is a means to greater comprehension. "Students working alone can complete simple assignments, learn simple procedures and information, and engage in well-learned behaviors. When new and complex knowledge and skills need to be mastered or extraordinary effort is needed however, learning groups are necessary" (Johnson and Johnson 2004, 8).

Michael: I read the phrase *extraordinary effort* as trying to digest and regurgitate a thirty-word vocabulary list for *Of Mice and Men*. It just makes good sense to encourage the students to participate in the teaching as well as the learning.

Sara: Classroom performance is active learning, the flip side of which makes me tired just thinking about it. As educator Harvey Daniels says, "Passive learning isn't just wrong because it is boring, it is wrong because it doesn't work" (Daniels and Bizar 1998).

Performance learning keeps kids engaged. Engagement in school can be the difference between dropping out and hanging in there. Group work and performance, oral performance, Web and printed publication—all encourage peer approval and build community in the classroom as kids work in teams. Teamwork gives them a safe opportunity to question one another as they build word and subject matter comprehension. We have all heard kids observe, "No one cares what I think." Putting learning into action gives students an audience for their learning.

If putting students in groups enhances relationships and relationships enhance learning, psychological health, and social skills, then building performance learning into your classroom design will help you meet your literacy goals and help students become better citizens beyond their time in the classroom. Isn't that our goal, after all—to foster interactive thinkers rather than solitary crossword solvers?

We have also found that collaboration works especially well in the ELL classroom. Given the opportunity to help each other out on a writing assignment not only shares the learning experience but builds a classroom culture of cooperation toward the assignment. This harnesses the logical propensity of second language learners to seek the familiarity of their fellow first language speakers toward your classroom's vocabulary and writing goals.

Michael: I was working with some seventh-grade students in Shanghai writing a definition poem for the Big Word (see Chapter 8) ***family***. The students became animated while trying to come up with a word that described *family* for them. "What's the thing under a bridge—it holds up a house, you know, like a pole, they're tall . . . column!" one from the group shouted. Their line became: *Family is like a column under a bridge.*

Sara: The word they were working on was *family*—but I bet they never forget the word ***column***.

Michael: Exactly.

We echo Isabel Beck's advice, "Written context lacks many of the features of oral language that support learning new word meanings, such as intonation, body language, and shared physical surroundings. As such, the text is a far less effective vehicle for learning new words than oral language" (Beck, McKeown, and Kucan 2002).

Embedding the new word into some sort of original oral presentation entices the student to use the new vocabulary in context with words that the student already knows and is comfortable with, rather than decoding context from a text that is as unfamiliar as the new word.

This book is really an outgrowth of our work with students to improve literacy through classroom performance as described in our book *Outspoken! How to Improve Writing and Speaking Skills Through Poetry Performance* (Holbrook and Salinger 2006) and in Sara's book on performance with younger elementary students, *Wham! It's a Poetry Jam* (Holbrook 2002), along with our work writing definition poems.

Sara: Me with my book for intermediate readers, *By Definition: Poems of Feelings* (Holbrook 2003), and *Practical Poetry: A Non-Standard Approach to Meeting Content Standards* (Holbrook 2005).

Michael: My book, *Well Defined: Vocabulary in Rhyme* (Salinger 2009), is a collection of delightfully (if I say so myself) humorous definition poems for SAT-level vocabulary words.

One of the seven comprehension strategies of a successful reader, as documented in *Mosaic of Thought* (Keene and Zimmermann 2007), is the ability to come up with images for what is being read. Teaching vocabulary and image-evoking techniques side by side seems to us to be a winning combination. Adding performance to the mix not only provides a word/symbol relationship for the students (listeners and performers) but also facilitates immediate assessment by the instructor and peers encouraging the students with an authentic reason to discuss the new words being introduced.

Who We Are

As performance poets and teaching artists, we have never really counted the number of students we work with every year. Let's just say the total would be significant (probably approaching 100,000, give or take a couple sleeping in the back of the room). Over the past twenty years, we've worked with writers ranging in age from carpet-remnant-sitting ankle biters to blue-rinse octogenarians in community education classrooms. We have come to see poetry and performance as not only an art product(s), but also a means to better communication skills. Poetry is distilled language. Just as writers of other genres do, the poet strives to communicate an idea.

To understand why two poets would choose to take four years to research, design, and test strategies for improving the vocabularies of young writers, we turn to that Amherst poetic diva Emily Dickinson, who stated, "*I hesitate which word to take, as I can take but few and each must be the chiefest . . .*" (Johnson 1958). The fact that spell-check finds ***chiefest*** to be a suspect word itself notwithstanding, Ms. Dickenson's dilemma is one with which all writers can empathize. We have all been in that pencil-tapping, cursor-staring place, searching our brains and dictionaries for just the right word. As teachers we are continually responding to students' pleas, "What's the word for . . . ?"

Our goal with each and every one of our students is not simply to coach them in writing poetry but to truly help them improve their communication skills by incorporating the benefits of poetry, along with other genres of creative nonfiction, and performance into the way they express themselves.

Sara: To help them be precise and concise.

Michael: Remembering that communication is a two-way street.

Sara: Speaking and listening is how we understand each other. It is how we learn about our world and how to function therein.

Michael: Therein?

Sara: I worked for eight years as the director of communications for a mega law firm before entering the field of education. What can I say?

Michael: And I worked at various manufacturing jobs, ending up as a quality engineer.

Which is all to say, what we bring to the classroom is not only our experience as poets and teaching artists but our combined knowledge of the dynamic communications requirements for success in the business world, a major component of which is the ability to acquire and employ a constant flow of new words.

Sara: Where but in a law firm would I have learned to be able to slip a word like ***adjudicate*** into a conversation?

Michael: Where else but in a machine shop would I have learned how to use a word like ***microfinish*** with fluency?

Sara: Fluency. To quote Emily again, now there's a word to "lift your hat to."

Michael: Didn't she say that about the word ***phosphorescence***?

Sara: Showoff.

Our classroom experience has taught us that the more students discussed the clear and implied meanings of words, putting the unfamiliar words in the context of their own language through discussion, writing, and classroom performance, the more they were able to expand their vocabularies, as evidenced in their writing. Like you, we want our students to be successful, fluent communicators, especially for the 87.5 percent of their lifetimes they will spend outside a classroom.

We began our venture into vocabulary instruction by reviewing what educational scholars and researchers suggest, studying curriculums that have been developed, and talking to classroom teachers all across the country. Our intention was not to develop a comprehensive vocabulary strategy across content areas and grade levels but rather to offer a variety of tools that teachers can employ in their overall approach to vocabulary instruction.

Based on thirty years of research, Beck and other educators have established three features of effective vocabulary instruction:

1. frequent encounters with the words
2. richness of instruction
3. extension of word use beyond the classroom (Beck, McKeown, and Kucan 2002)

In *Bringing Words to Life*, Beck, McKeown, and Kucan define a robust approach to vocabulary as one that "involves directly explaining the meaning of words along with thought-provoking, playful and interactive follow-up" (2002). Unfortunately, one rather discouraging situation we discovered in our classroom research was that despite various research-based pleas for teachers to be more "playful" and "interactive" in their vocabulary instruction (Whitaker 2008; Allen 1999; Beck, McKeown, and Kucan 2002), too many reluctant students are still being driven to learn words independently through methods that have been proven not to work. In fact, we became suspicious that the classroom methods (worksheets, lists, quizzes) being used to teach vocabulary might be the precise reason kids were not engaging in the process.

So, how to hook those resistant learners? Alfred Tatum states, "Students who are not used to providing authentic responses to texts will resist doing so until they begin to trust that their responses will be valued and respected" (2005). Our classroom experience has demonstrated that performance can help to fill this need of students to feel that their ideas are respected. In order to combat a youth culture that too often elevates *not* knowing.

Delivering Vigorous Vocabulary Instruction

Embedding vocabulary instruction within multiple writing genres already being taught in the classroom and strengthening this learning through performance, we believe, adds to a deeper understanding of words. In this book we offer a variety of lessons that show you how to use genre writing, collaboration, and performance to help your kids build strong and lively vocabularies. Each lesson follows a basic teachable pattern, carefully tweaked for each individual lesson. The master lesson plan goes like this.

Lesson Process

❶ **Share** samples of the chosen writing genre with your students by reading it out loud. In each chapter, we provide mentor texts for every genre and subcategory we introduce. You may use our samples or you may decide to choose other models.

❷ **Discuss** the qualities of the genre with the class. What are the conventions of a set of instructions? How does the formality of a business letter compare with casualness of a journal entry? What kinds of words are best used and in what sequence when writing directions? Discuss structures or patterns utilized specific to any particular genre.

❸ **Model** the process by co-creating one of these word-pieces along with your students, with you scribing their suggestions on the board or projector. Leave this example on the board while students work on their own pieces. Don't skip this step!

As Stephanie Harvey says, "In real estate it's location, location, location—in teaching it is model, model, and model"(Harvey and Daniels 2009). Now, this may seem like just one more thing to add to an increasingly jammed school day, but it is really about going slow to go fast. We can't just command kids to think and read and write—we must *show* them how. At this stage of each lesson, the teacher solicits student input, so the students are collaborating during the composing, discussing, and debating as the text is created. As you work, be sure to look into the second and third meanings of the word. Image evoking and leading questions are encouraged; we want to instill the concepts of collaboration and playful debate as part of the creative process.

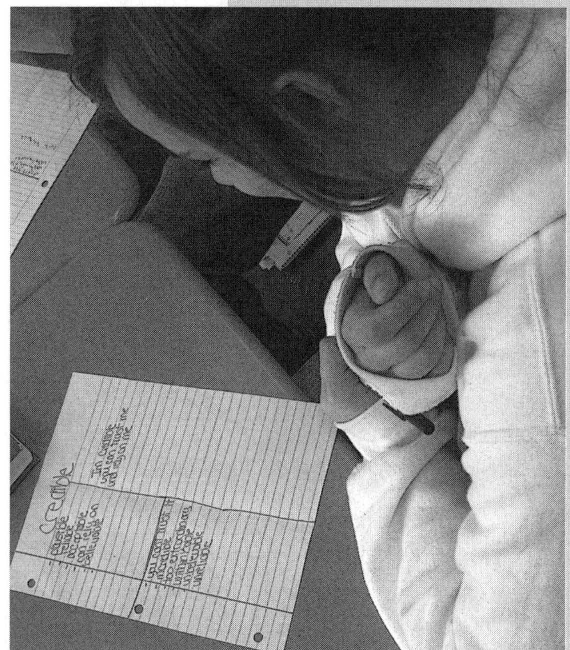

Figure 1.9 *An eighth grader creates a* **credible** *prewrite.*

❹ **Choose and collaborate.** Choose or assign vocabulary words (see Chapter 2, "Choosing the Words") for your writers or groups of writers. The more student choice and relevance the words reflect, the better the chance that kids will bring energy to learning them. We believe collaboration is a sure road to success and encourage you to have students work in groups of two or three. Don't hesitate to assign duplicate words to several groups; as different perspectives on words arise, so does the opportunity for more discussion and deeper understanding.

❺ **Provide** vocabulary research materials for your students. Ideally this should not be limited to a classroom set of dictionaries. Take a look back at our ideas about Researching Words in the Digital Age (on page xi). Remember to promote checking with multiple sources and digging into secondary meanings of the vocabulary words. Encourage kids to use glossaries, handouts, websites, examples of how the word is used in different contexts, and of course, to take time to discuss meanings with partners or other experts before composing. This inquisitive mode of research can be modeled during the crafting portion of this procedure in step three.

❻ **Write.** Provide writing time in class. These sessions need not be long, drawn-out affairs—ten to fifteen minutes per word should suffice. We'll have time for revision and creating a Version 2, later. Some students will want to break out after the collaboration (still sharing the contents of the Cheat Sheet) to write independently. This is perfectly fine. If students are writing in groups or even solo, expect and encourage a low murmur of discussion during the writing process as students confer to clarify meanings.

❼ **Turn and talk.** Have students share their writing out loud within their groups—or in pairs or small groups if they have been working solo. This provides an opportunity for first edits and informal peer review, preparing the students to present their work in front of the rest of the class, a stepping-stone and rehearsal before facing the whole group.

❽ **Perform.** Invite students to present their word-pieces to the whole class. If they have been working in small groups, the whole group participates in the performance. This could be as simple as alternating lines read aloud or as involved as full-costumed choreography. We'll give some tips for pairing particular types of performance with certain genres that we have found successful as we introduce them. The important part here is that the students know their work will culminate in front of a live audience, adding an authentic reason for best effort.

❾ **Assess.** Lead the class in a discussion of the writing and performance they have just experienced. Ask kids what they think the new vocabulary word means, what it doesn't mean. Was the writing and performance successful in communicating meaning—if this is the second or third presentation of the word, how was it different from those that preceded it? (See *Outspoken!* for performance assessment rubrics [Holbrook and Salinger 2006].)

❿ **Hazards.** If there are predictable problems with these lessons, we will help you identify how to avoid them. For example, one stumbling block that can occur across all genres is inferior research resources. In order for our students to create rich writing we must provide them with more than an explanatory sentence or, worse, a single synonym. We are asking our kids to wrap their new vocabulary in a thick quilt of expressive writing and to satisfactorily provide an example of a writing format as well as a definition. What should be a fun and challenging lesson can be downright frustrating when underprovisioned. We'll address other genre specific hazards as we present them.

⓫ **Extra credit.** Some of these exercises lend themselves to bigger and bolder presentations incorporating special technologies or grander performances—we'll make some suggestions as the opportunities arise.

Sara: We are providing you with a means to reteach writing forms with powerful words as their subjects.

Michael: Along with a sampling of words kids are learning in grades 4 through 10, the words that are included with the exercises are divided roughly into two levels—harder and easier—allowing you to differentiate depending on the needs of your own classroom.

Sara: It's time to change the boring vocabulary lesson paradigm.

Michael: We found out exactly how ingrained these assumptions were when we told friends that we were working on a vocabulary acquisition book.

Sara: They responded with sighs and sympathy, as if we'd simultaneously contracted an unfortunate disease. And these are people who are decades out of school.

Michael: We have a new simile to suggest for vocabulary lesson. Fun!

Sara: As in, "It's about as fun as a vocabulary lesson."

Michael: Okay. Let's get to work.

Choosing the Words

Michael: Here's a math quiz: If Merriam-Webster claims 476,000 entries in its unabridged dictionary, and you take those words and divide them by thirteen years of schooling and then you divide again by the number of weeks in the school year, how many new words do you need to teach your class next Monday?

Sara: Where'd I put that calculator . . . ?

Michael: Don't forget to factor in the 700,000 definitions and 143,000 etymologies.

Sara: You lost me at 476,000.

Michael: Well, the correct answer is 2,644.4 words per day, assuming a 180-day school year.

The sheer number of words that exist in the English language is (in a word) overwhelming. As language arts teachers, we obviously do not need to teach every one. But we do strive to make our students lovers of words, immersing them in rich descriptions, urging them to play with language—to experiment with and investigate unfamiliar words. We want them to gather and own the best, the most powerful, the most generative words around. Now, compound this with research showing that students need to acquire approximately 4,000 words a year to build this kind of vigorous vocabulary (Nagy, Herman, and Anderson 1985) and the task seems beyond Herculean.

With so many words to choose from, where do we begin, at what grade level, and in which content area? And do we teach the new words before a unit, as we go along, or simply view word knowledge as an assessment tool?

Before we can choose a method of teaching new words, we have to determine which to teach. In her book, *Word Play*, Sandra Whitaker tells us that "95 percent of words on a page are comprised of basic vocabulary—words like *is*, *her*, *do*, the other five percent of words tend to carry meaning" (2008).

Sara: Okay, 5 percent. That seems a little less impossible.

Michael: Still, a lot of choices to be made. Five percent of the text in your average 300-page novel still amounts to a pile of words.

If you accept the premise that few people really need to know that ***oxter*** is a synonym for *armpit*, how do you decide which words your students *do* need to know?

Classification of Words

To help you select which words would be most beneficial for your students to understand, we adapted Isabel Beck's tiered system for classifying vocabulary words. Using this framework, you can more easily sort through words and sort them into three categories (Beck, McKeown, and Kucan 2002).

1. **Tier One: Basic Words.** Words we use in everyday conversation. These are concrete image words, nouns such as ***cup***, ***lamp***, ***bird***, and verbs like ***run***, ***jump***, and ***sleep***. It's important to note that even though these

words are basic for communication, many are new to our students and may include synonyms for words they already know.

Cup = container, goblet, chalice

Bird = parrot, sparrow, pelican

Jump = pounce, plunge, bound

2. **Tier Two: Concept Words.** These are bigtime meaning-making words that often represent abstractions, and are likely to be encountered in multiple contexts. These are words such as ***reflection***, ***migrate***, ***baffled***, ***swagger***, ***reform***, ***eclipse***, ***summation***. These are words that are not so archaic as to have fallen out of use (such as ***oxter*** for *armpit*) or so content-area-specific that they are rarely used in conversation (***chrysalis***, ***zygote***). Students may expect to encounter concept words with some frequency across content areas, in literature, on the news, or in the workplace.

3. **Tier Three: Content-Specific/Academic Words**. These words are directly related to content-area learning. It is into this category that we put words such as ***longitude***, ***ovum***, ***molecular***, ***isthmus***. These academic words, while integral to our content-area learning, rarely wander outside of the classroom or the lab to land at the dinner table or on the shop floor. They are specific descriptors, many of which are compounded and technical and are best taught before or along with a content-specific lesson.

Classifying words according to these three tiers provides you with the perspective to perhaps choose a few from each tier to teach independently. Naturally, the classification process is open to argument.

Sara: Take the word *eclipse*. Some might say that is an academic word describing a solar event, but it is also a concept word as one thing may *eclipse* another.

Michael: I thought *eclipse* was a gum.

Sara: Gum, a basic word that is also a content-area/academic word that is also a concept word, as in you are ***gumming*** up the lesson here, Salinger.

How you classify words for use in your classroom will depend on the students' grade level and of course may span one or more tiers. Particularly in our literature classrooms, we will want to focus on basic and concept words. You may wish to draw students into this discussion; classifying new words as basic, concept, or content specific/academic will help them appreciate the authentic reasons to learn new words.

Michael: I might add another category—Bizzaro Words. I'm thinking of ***ululation***, a word out of *Lord of the Flies*.

Sara: The first time I heard ***woofers*** and ***tweeters*** used to describe audio equipment, it made me laugh out loud.

Michael: Some words are just fun to say. And they are even more fun to say if you know what they mean.

Sara: You mean like the civil war weapon, the ***breechloader***?

Michael: I thought *breechloader* was a synonym for an unexpected loud noise.

Fun is not necessarily a word first associated with vocabulary lessons. However, by helping kids to look at words through direct application to their daily lives, we make the learning more authentic. And if you can spark an argument about a word's potential use in the future, all the better. Arguments require active engagement on the parts of students, and that's what makes lessons more meaningful and memorable.

Of course we would never suggest that you eschew that third tier completely in favor of a vocabulary list composed solely of concept-carrying words. There are times when specific and technical vocabulary must be taught in order to comprehend a lesson. A class period on photosynthesis is not going to go very far without Tier Three words such as ***chlorophyll*** or ***glucose***. The same lesson may also provide an opportunity to introduce some pretty powerful Tier Two words: ***atmosphere***, ***reaction***, and ***pigment***, to name a few. We are simply suggesting that you keep your eyes peeled for and exploit the opportunities to teach concept-carrying vocabulary words when they arise.

The lessons in this book will help students commit their new vocabulary into their schema as they collaborate to form meanings for unfamiliar words by inserting them into stories, letters, and poems surrounded by words they already understand.

> ***Michael:*** A word like ***investment*** can be utilized across subject matter yet maintain a core meaning that stays true as it is employed.
>
> ***Sara:*** I know that somewhere in my academic career I had to learn the names of different architectural bits and pieces of the Globe Theater—there's an *investment* that paid scant dividends.
>
> ***Michael:*** Exactly. When putting together our vocabulary lessons we need to focus on words that have overarching capabilities, not ones that are so narrow, so discipline bound that our students may never encounter them again.

Basic, concept, and even some content-area-specific academic words will naturally lend themselves to the personifications our students will use in defining their meanings. The creative and fun thought processes needed when writing and presenting an obituary for ***chloroplast***, for example, will surround this and other highly specific terms with words familiar to and of the students' own choosing—certainly a whole lot more memorable than a single-sentence definition copied from the glossary in the back of the book.

Word Choice

Many states and districts mandate week-to-week word lists totally unrelated to the curriculum students are studying. Sometimes this is done in hopeful preparation for some distant state test, the ACT, or SAT exam. This approach is the academic equivalent of gruel funneled down students' throats. For our kids there is no apparent reason to partake, no aroma of inquiry to get their mouths watering, and no lasting nutritional value that will help them grow. We should not be surprised when they relieve themselves of such lessons as quickly as possible, and forget those random words forthwith. Bleh.

"People who have large vocabularies tend to be intrigued with words," Beck reminds us (Beck, McKeown, and Kucan 2002). So, therein lays the first and most important challenge—getting students who are mostly intrigued with video games and texting abbreviations to become intrigued with words. If our goal is a love of language, let's face it: force-feeding through word lists is not going to get us there. Instead, we need to let students help identify the new words they will be learning. Nothing sets a task in motion faster than giving students a voice in choosing what they will study. Whether it is the solar system, the inner workings of a toaster, or a vocabulary lesson, kids will be more motivated to learn when they study what they really want to know. Having students identify challenging words in the course of study provides them with a sense of ownership in the lesson.

While there is not one best way to choose words for vocabulary lessons, there are some profoundly ineffective ways and a random word list is one of them. By this we mean word lists generated with no association to classroom units and reading.

Ben (bobbling-a-marshmallow-on-a-stick Ben from Chapter 1) is now in fourth grade. He's a good student, scoring consistently well on state benchmark proficiency tests.

> ***Sara:*** Is this where I get to brag that last year he received a perfect score on the social studies portion of the test?
>
> ***Michael:*** You might want to mention that Ben is our grandson. It ups the reader's tolerance level for braggadocio.
>
> ***Sara:*** His teacher was so excited, she called the house.
>
> ***Michael:*** Okay, that's enough.

Every week Ben completes his homework assignment as per instruction—he puts vocabulary words from a list into a sentence.

Each sentence is complete and logical. But does this sentence toward the end of the page, "My dad is sometimes strict but mostly fun," actually define ***strict***? Can we tell if Ben understands what *strict* means and does not mean? Not really. Still, this exercise is being repeated in classrooms and kitchen tables in the forms of worksheets and homework assignments for students in grades 4 through 12 all over the country, week after week.

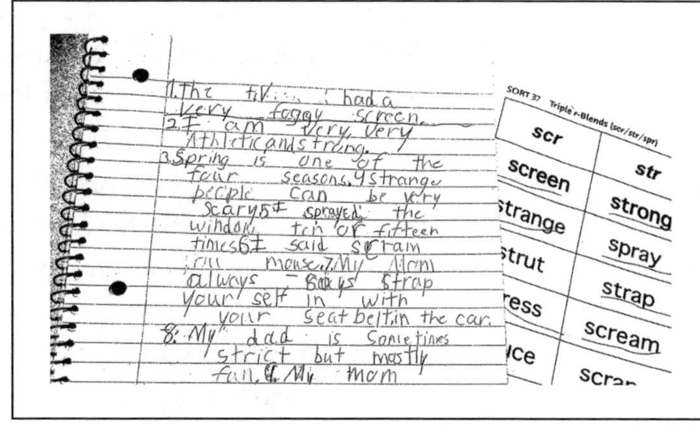

Figure 2.1 *Sentence Definitions for Fourth-Grade Vocabulary*

Michael: Remember that one ninth-grade teacher who chose words out of a novel and typed them up with one-word synonyms for students to memorize? ***Strident*** was defined as ***harsh***, leading one student to this sentence definition, "Cleveland weather is strident in the winter."

Sara: Word lists don't work for me. I've tried to memorize those lists of two- and three-letter words guaranteed to improve my score in Scrabble. No can do.

Michael: Let's face it, word lists don't work for many of us, your Scrabble score notwithstanding.

Sara: Don't get personal.

In the course of writing this book, we were lucky enough to teach alongside some very inspiring veteran teachers, each of whom took a personalized path to building their students' vocabularies.

We walked into Libby Royko's Eastlake Middle School eighth-grade language arts classroom while the students were collectively reading *To Kill a Mockingbird*. Aware that this was challenging text for her students, Libby encouraged the kids to let her know when they encountered an unfamiliar word, whereupon she would write the word on the board. There were three sections of board in her classroom and on the day we arrived, two were crammed with words.

Libby reported that the kids were very engaged in the text, but every paragraph presented unknown words. The words on the board were words the students had self-selected as difficult, not just words she had downloaded from some prepackaged lesson plan on the novel. It would have been impossible for her to introduce all of those words in advance to prep them for the reading.

Using herself as a reading resource, Libby explained each new word in the context of her students' reading and then wrote it on the board, creating a word wall dense with chalky annotations. Don't misinterpret, Libby is an experienced and talented teacher, she knows that simply posting the words does not mean her students actually understand the words. But her main goal in having students identify the unfamiliar words was to help them not get so bogged down in strange words that they would miss out on a good story.

Still, there were all those words—good words, usable words. What a shame to let them get washed away by the custodian before the students could gain a deeper understanding that would enable putting the vocabulary to use in their own lives.

So, collaborating with Libby, our solution was to have the students help us choose fifteen of the words to incorporate into our writing exercises. Working as a team, we guided the selection of these words from the blackboard, weighing their conceptual meaning-making power by asking ourselves a simple question: How likely was it that our students would encounter the word again outside of this novel? We were looking for high-value, Tier Two, interdisciplinary words. By performing this vocabulary triage we were able to turn our insurmountable word wall into a manageable task. We chose words like ***baffled***, ***fluctuation***, ***nebulous***, ***reminiscent***, ***fanatical***, ***perplexed***, ***morbid***, ***strident***, ***malevolent***, and ***articulate*** for deeper study.

This culling allowed us to take the time to teach this vocabulary more deeply and, through our lessons, to reapply this fresh vocabulary in new circumstances. We took those words down off the board, put shoes on them, and let them walk, talk, think, and dance.

> ***Michael:*** I think one writer put a uniform with epaulets on *strident*.
>
> ***Sara:*** And that was before they even knew what ***epaulets*** were.
>
> ***Michael:*** One good word leads to another.

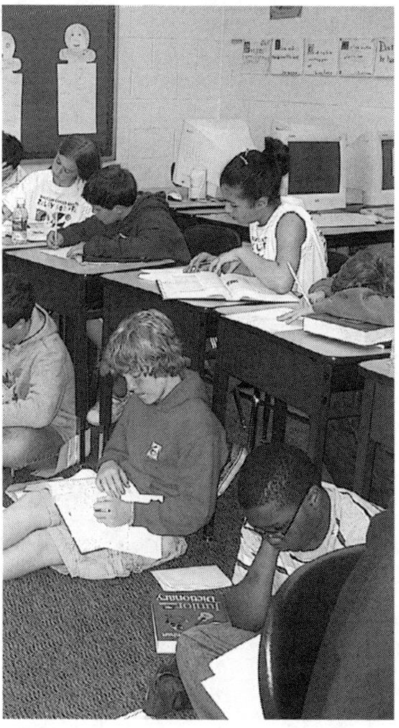

Figure 2.2 *Sixth-Grade Math Students Writing Their Way to a Better Vocabulary*

In Mark Kevesdy's sixth-grade math classroom and in his colleagues Laurel Beck and Brent Illenberger's science labs, new words are introduced before the unit. It would be impossible to discuss the digestive tract without at least a passing knowledge of the word ***esophagus***, for instance. These content-area teachers understand the shortcomings of the learning-words-in-context strategy where technical language is concerned. The surrounding text most often lends no clues for the new words cropping up in front of the student. So these savvy instructors frontload their lessons making sure their students aren't blindsided when encountering words such as ***biotic*** or ***equiangular***.

It is important to define these topic-specific vocabulary words beforehand in order to successfully teach a unit on cellular reproduction or the area of a triangle, but there are also plenty of words germane to these subjects that carry conceptual meaning outside of graph paper and Petri dishes. ***Denominator***, ***random***, ***ratio***, ***diffusion***, ***metamorphic*** all carry significance across disciplines and nurturing an understanding of these terms in these multiple circumstances is a key component of vigorous vocabulary instruction.

Fourth-grade teacher Teena Mitchell knew the importance of selecting high-powered vocabulary while she gathered words for her unit on the rain forest. Through research, collaboration, writing, and performing, the students were able to construct word meanings. In her classroom the students' written text utilized words such as ***canopy***, ***banana***,

precipitation, ***snake***, ***frog***, and ***reptile***. The students' written artifacts became a tool for Teena to assess their understanding of the unit of study as well as their grasp of the terms being defined.

Our research brought us back to Katie Lufkin's sixth-grade language arts classroom several times. Her practice was to pull challenge words from the novels that the students were reading, both by preselection and student suggestion. The novels included titles such as *Stargirl*, *The Watsons Go to Birmingham—1963*, and *The Outsiders*. Each of these books was rich with concept words, the definitions of which not only helped to explain the stories but also what was happening right out in the hall. Words such as ***prejudice***, ***conformity***, ***minority***, and ***tolerance*** engaged students immediately in deep discussion as they talked over how such words could be extracted from the fictional texts and applied to real-world situations.

We visited sixth-grade social studies teachers Robbie Tupa and Angela Randjelovic's classrooms on a couple of different occasions—once during a unit on the feudal system and once while they were studying desert terrain. Together, these two educators identified vocabulary that would benefit students in advance of each of the units and then taught those words in a variety of ways during the units, culminating with a quiz at the end for an assessment.

Christine Landaker-Charbonneau's eighth-grade class in Milton, Massachusetts, has a permanent word wall with words organized in alphabetical order. The words have arisen from the student's independent reading and from text that they are reading as a group. Unfamiliar words are suggested both by the

Figure 2.3 *Christine and Her Eighth-Grade Classroom Word Wall*

students and by Christine herself. The word wall is a dynamic part of the classroom, constantly in a state of flux.

Again and again we witnessed teachers selecting their vocabulary lists based on the power of the word's conceptual meaning—dynamic Tier Two vocabulary capable of leaping from subject to subject in a single bound. We have seen, even when the lesson at hand requires us to get a bit technical, there are always opportunities to introduce some over-achieving words.

Understanding that there is not one right way to choose the words, we also needed some words typically taught at the middle school level that would work with our lessons. Through classroom research and reading, we assembled some Tier One and Tier Two words, which appear toward the end of each chapter. Since this book is for teachers spanning grades 4 through 10, we further subdivided these lists into Easier and Harder words.

Sara: Don't stop there. Choose words from your class' units of study.

Michael: And let your students have a voice in choosing the words.

High Definition Through Explanatory Writing

"Just the facts, Ma'am." (or, "Sir")

The words of television pioneer *Dragnet* detective Joe Friday are echoed by teachers in classrooms all across curriculums, school systems, and the country as they coach their students through explanatory writing assignments with stern admonitions to tell the truth, the whole truth, and nothing but the truth. The truth about Abraham Lincoln, Friday's game, shark attacks. The truth revealed through letters, instructions, directions, how-tos, sequence descriptions, news reports, obituaries, and interviews. In this genre, writers are warned that an editorial detective will be watching for clear statements of fact, detailed descriptions, and flags will be raised for even a flinch of fiction. The writer will stick to the facts, OR ELSE!

Michael: Or else what?

Sara: You know.

Michael: Could you be more specific?

Sara: That's the point.

Figure 3.1 *Sixth graders confer prior to performance.*

Explanatory writing is all about specifics, the what-ups, how-tos, and why-fors. Writers may organize these nonfiction specifics into various text types. For students, learning how to organize their details in a logical manner is not a process they will master on their first attempt. These thinking processes must be practiced repeatedly to attain mastery of the skills necessary to make factual data comprehensible.

Both of us, having grown into writing careers from the business world, are acutely aware of the importance of being able to put what we have seen not only into words, but just the right words in a specific order. Being skilled at precise language is perhaps one of the most useful lessons we can give our students in preparing them to graduate into an ever-changing world.

Sara: During my tenure as director of communications for a mega-law firm, we often had to be exhaustively specific, writing in what we called "SEC" language. That meant providing descriptions of compliances, deadlines, and corporate actions that would pass examination by the Securities and Exchange Commission. Of course, then we would conclude every written transmission with some kind of "this is exactly how it is *as of this time*" language that would let everyone out the litigation back door if what we had just said turned out to be false the next day.

Michael: Or the next hour?

Sara: I think sometimes we were splitting seconds.

Michael: Working as a quality engineer for many years I learned the importance of getting to the root of a matter as precisely and concisely as possible. If I were to meander about with ancillary details without getting to the point, folks would have simply just gotten up and left the meeting room. Time is money in the real world. Helping our students to craft explanatory writing that presents facts in an orderly manner will pay off.

Sara: I take it they would not have been very patient with editorializing?

Michael: There is no artistic interpretation in machining that doesn't hazard losing a finger.

Having well-honed explanatory writing skills isn't just an idle practice designed to help students triumph over achievement tests, although it will aid there, also. This is writing that will help students in their adult careers and as community members because not only is it a writing skill, it is a thinking process. And having access to a broad and precise vocabulary is the best route to the kind of effective explanatory writing that will help students succeed throughout their lives.

In this chapter, vocabulary words become the subject of news accounts. Vocabulary words fill out job applications. Students may exercise their explanatory writing skills through writing business letters signed by words such as ***inept***. A few words even tragically die, leaving behind biographical death notices.

Each lesson contains a writing sample, which may be combined with the Collaboration Cheat Sheet (Appendix A) to help students organize their thoughts.

Writing a News Report

This Just In: Words Make the News

Most news articles begin with a strong lead containing the major facts (who, what, where, when, and why) and follow with supporting details in decreasing degree of importance, an inverted pyramid style. This style not only fits the skimming practices of the reading audience, but also the needs of the layout editor who simply cuts from the bottom to squeeze in the news that prints to fit. Unlike narrative writing, this is one place where students don't have to concern themselves with a strong conclusion.

What they do have to concern themselves with is sticking to the facts—even in a made-up news report such as what happened when ***cataclysmic*** made its entrance into Riverside Middle School. (See Appendix B for a copy of this article in a reproducible format.) In an era where the fuzzy line between news reporting and editorializing seems to be getting blurrier by the news hour, it is good for students to recognize the difference between fact and opinion.

This is where we started our discussion about the qualities of straight news reporting in Mark Kevesdy's sixth-grade math class. First we projected this story for a read-aloud.

Sample News Article for *Cataclysmic*

Riverside, OH—*Cataclysmic* ran through the front door Monday morning and straight into the trophy case at Riverside Middle School, scattering glass shards in the hallway and injuring fourteen students before tripping over his own feet and setting off the fire alarms causing the sprinkler system to go off and flooding the band room.

"I never saw such a messy, disastrous entry into the lobby," said Principal Ms. Sandra Smith. "*Cataclysmic* is a total wreck. We're very lucky there were no fatalities."

When asked to explain his behavior, *Cataclysmic* just shook his head and agreed that his actions were in fact dangerous. "Did you see all that broken glass?"

Principal Smith predicts that it will take days to restore order in the lobby and drain the band room and weeks to construct a new trophy case. Meantime, *Cataclysmic* will be serving detention for one month where he pledges that he will learn to become a productive student and how to enter the school without causing devastation, harming himself or others.

We noted that the story led with the W's (who, what, where, when) and then we examined the article for opinion words. All the opinions were those of Principal Smith and not the opinions of the reporter. The reporter does not admonish *Cataclysmic* to become a more productive student, he pledges to do so himself. We identified synonyms (***devastation***,

disastrous, ***dangerous***) buried within the story that helped define the word. We looked for an antonym (***productive***) that further helped to define the word. We noted that all news stories have a dateline that briefly describes where and when the story took place.

Sara: News reporters do have biases. So do editors.

Michael: Yes, but traditionally they are limited to exhibiting those biases though which stories they choose to report and publish. No "I think," or "in my opinion," stated or implied.

Sara: Publish or broadcast. Students have viewed a lot more television reporting than they have read newspapers.

Michael: True. Which is why while our examples here were written for publication, you may wish instead to have students draft news reports with the intent of using them for broadcast or even podcast.

Sara: Which is exactly what we did when it came to the performance portion of the lesson—we pretended that we were reading the stories on the radio, using a pencil holder for a microphone.

After we discussed the qualities of a news story with Mark's students, each table group of four students chose two math vocabulary words from a basket. This was a lesson-learned approach after we first had asked them to choose from a list on the board, which resulted in almost everyone's choosing the word ***random***. Because our goal was that everyone in the class should understand all of the words, we had to intervene to make sure all of the words were selected.

Sara: Are you implying that sometimes our first approach to a lesson doesn't work?

Michael: Implying nothing. I'm totally outing the fact that these lessons were in a constant state of flux as we tested and learned.

Sara: What we are sharing is what worked best for us and our students. Please don't hesitate to make adjustments to meet your classroom goals.

Directing students to choose their words, even by allowing them to draw them from a basket, engenders a sense of ownership with the words before they even begin writing.

Certain (by James) and ***Random*** (by Habukka) (see Figures 3.2a and 3.2b) were the subjects of two news reports from Mark Kevesdy's sixth-grade math students. As the news accounts were read aloud, we also learned that no one knows what ***Uncertainty*** will do next, that when ***Chance*** (whose odds were only 50/50) lost all his money in Vegas, his wife, *Certain*, dumped him, ***Experimental*** had been changed into a genetic freak because of an accident involving gamma radiation, and ***Probability*** could predict how possible it is for a hurricane to hit Los Angeles. The articles were fun to hear aloud and after each we asked, "Now what does this word mean?" of the listeners. As part of a peer assessment, we also discussed whether the lead answered who, what, where, when and if the article was straight news reporting, with all opinions being in quotes.

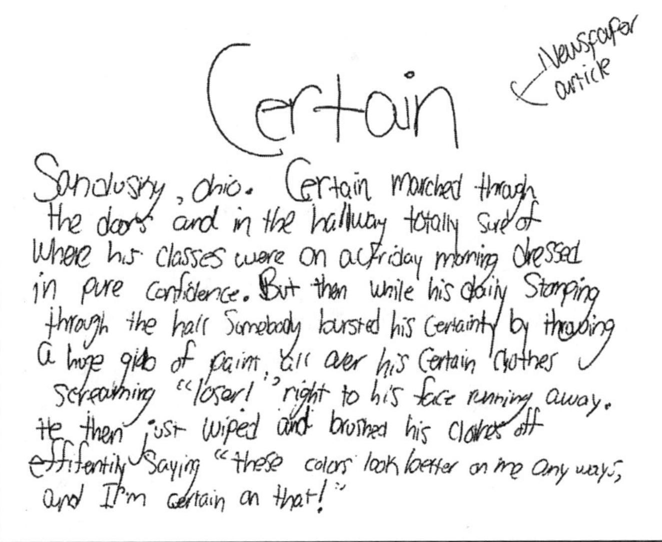
Certain

Newspaper article

Sandusky, Ohio. Certain marched through the doors and in the hallway totally sure of where his classes were on a Friday morning dressed in pure confidence. But then while his daily stomping through the hall somebody bursted his certainty by throwing a huge glob of paint all over his certain clothes screaming "loser!" right to his face running away. He then just wiped and brushed his clothes off effifentily saying "these colors look better on me any ways, and I'm certain on that!"

Figure 3.2a **Certain** *by James*

Figure 3.2b **Random** *by Hebukka*

Sea side hill Florida.- random Hijacked an air force stealth bomber and crashed it in his nebors garage for no reason at all this happens this tuesday.

"This is going to cost billions of dollars to the air force" said Genaral willson. When the judge asked him why random did it he he plainly said "I don't know". His neibor certain said "He could never give precies explanations."

Sara: Excitement was running so high that table groups were stealing words from other tables after they finished so that they could continue making up *random* stories.

Michael: What would you say the *probability* is that sixth graders would want to steal vocabulary words?

Sara: I might have ***predicted*** that to be a big zero until I saw it myself.

For extra credit you may wish to have the kids collaborate to convert their news articles into a full newspaper either on paper, in online podcasts, or news flashes to be read with morning announcements.

Michael: Fake news stories can ***certainly*** be attention getters. Look what happened with Orson Welles' fabled broadcast, *War of the Worlds*.

Sara: How about a new series, War of the Words?

Writing Business Letters

Sincerely, Vocabulary

When a voice on an answering machine, an IM exchange, or a text message just won't do, we rely on the old-fashioned standby, the business letter. The cover letter, the application, the inquiry—when we just have no choice but to put it in writing, we want to be taken seriously. A business letter is patterned writing, form and function combined to inform and often to elicit a response from the reader.

Of all the types of structured writing students are required to master, this might be one that actually lands them a summer internship, admission to college, or the all-important stay of execution. Being able to draft a professionally crafted business letter may mean the difference between landing a job or unemployment, being reimbursed or going uncompensated. Success in any number of real-world situations depends on the ability of a writer to appear competent by executing a solid business letter.

The advent of email has effectively replaced much of the day-to-day business correspondence, leaving only the most critical letter writing to actual paper and envelopes. Now that society has relegated only these most important letters to be stamped and deposited in actual inboxes, it is even more important that writers know how to get it right. This does not mean though, that the tools used in good explanatory writing should not come into play in the electronic age. The email you dash off to a friend when trying to pick a restaurant for lunch is not going to bear much resemblance to the letter you email to the department head and fifteen colleagues detailing a field trip proposal.

> ***Michael:*** While working with a fourth-grade class at Charles Lake Elementary in Cleveland, Ohio, I led the class in writing business letters to local luminaries requesting an interview with the students as a part of local history unit. The kids were thrilled when the replies started coming in—especially the ones mentioning the quality of the children's initial letter as a motivating factor in the decision to accept the invitation to be interviewed—a real-world payoff beneficial to the class project.

One of the days we visited Bay Middle School, social studies teachers Katie Lufkin and Sherri Deal were in the midst of a unit on Ancient Worlds and the Sahara Desert terrain in their sixth-grade social studies classrooms. Katie and Sherri had chosen a short list of vocabulary words for further study, which included: ***desert***, ***savanna***, ***migration***, ***Swahili***, ***barter***, ***oasis***, ***rain forest***, and ***clan***. We began by introducing the concept of writing a cover business letter for a job application and sharing an example that we had written, signed by a word that was unfamiliar to the sixth graders, *inept*. (See Appendix C for a copy of this letter in a reproducible format.)

Sample Business Letter for *Inept*

Inept
333 Slippery Street
Unskilled, USA

Factory Founder
444 Efficient Row
Successful, USA
September 1, 2003 (or 2008, I can't remember)

Dear Mr. Founder:

I would like to apply for the job of manager of your manufacturing plant in Successful, USA. I am not the least bit qualified for this position because I am unskilled and clumsy. If you are looking for an employee you can really count on, that couldn't possibly be me.

I feel I have a lot to contribute to your organization. I know how to stall any project and can't problem solve at all. I am neither competent nor skilled in any way. I never do as I am told and rarely can handle any project sent my way.

If you are looking for someone you can count on to always drop the ball, I am your person.

Thank you for your kind attention. If you wish to contact me, look my number up yourself.

Sincerely,
Inept

We used this model to discuss both the meaning of the word and to review the business letter format. We also discussed what kind of business letter this was; one in which the writer is seeking employment. Each table group was assigned two words and the students collaborated to complete the Collaboration Cheat Sheet (Appendix A). For this activity, we added an additional prewrite and had students complete a profile of their word as if it were filling out a job application form.

Michael: Just like you, sometimes we try things on the fly.

Sara: Like doubling down on the prewrite.

Michael: And this is one of those occurrences where the experiment really paid off!

Together with the students we formulated a list of typical job application questions such as: name, address, interests, experience, and goals, which were then written on the board. We prompted students by asking them: What extra details would we need in order to create a believable business letter for our vocabulary word? Where might this word live? What are its goals for the future? What are the word's strengths and weaknesses? The students worked in small groups to discuss their words and complete the job applications (see Figures 3.3a and 3.3b).

We had combined two classes for the writing and kids were at desks and on the floor engaged in vigorous research and discussion in order to

Desert

Name: Hollis Desert
Address: 109 Oasis Lane
City & State: Baren, Kenya
Age: 32
Interest & Experience:
Camel Rider
Survival Expert
Sand Storm Survivor
Sand Castle Expert
Dehidrated for 5 days
Able to withstand Extreme Heat
Goals:
Find an oasis
See a forest
Learn to swim
See a fish
Be in a large Crowd

Figure 3.3a *Gail's* **Desert** *Profile Details*

Hollis Desert
109 Oasis Lane
Baren, Kenya

Survival Kitts
88 Sandy Way
Deserted, Kenya

June 1, 2007

Dear Ms. Success,

I recently heard about your business, and decided my knowledge could help you out. I'm from the great Sahara Desert, and have had to learn ways to survive there. I am a great writer, and can write about your survival kits and books about how to survive. Please consider me for this position.

I have a lot of experience. In the desert, I learned to tame and ride camels for my transportation. I've survived dehidration for 5 straight days, 3 sand storms, and temperatures reaching up to 115 degrees Farenheit. I've mastered the art of sand castle sculpting, and have become a survival expert, though I want to expand my knowledge and make money through your company. I've also set goals for my dry life, like to find an oasis, see a forest, learn to swim, see fish, and be in a large crowd. As you can see, I'm quite experienced.

Please consider this letter, and get back to me soon. Thanks!

Sincerely,
Hollis Desert

Figure 3.3b *Gail's* **Desert** *Business Letter*

complete their applications. The four of us circulated to make sure the writers were on task. No problems there! Despite what appeared to be lively chaos, everyone was engaged, collaborating to complete the short applications. This made the letter writing easy as students then worked individually to give voice to the word people they had invented, following the standard business letter form. (See Figures 3.4a and 3.4b.)

The job applicants had hopes and goals as high as you would expect for sixth graders. Sam assumed the persona of Harry *Barter* (from Neptune) for whom the sky was no limit at all! He wanted to take his bartering skills to the outer limits of the solar system. His job application might look as if Sam (aka Harry Barter) was most interested in practicing his new signature, but his letter of application to his future boss, the owner of a trucking company, makes it clear that Sam knows the meaning of the word *barter*.

Since business letters don't readily adapt to an oral performance, we improvised again. For the final performance, the students conducted real

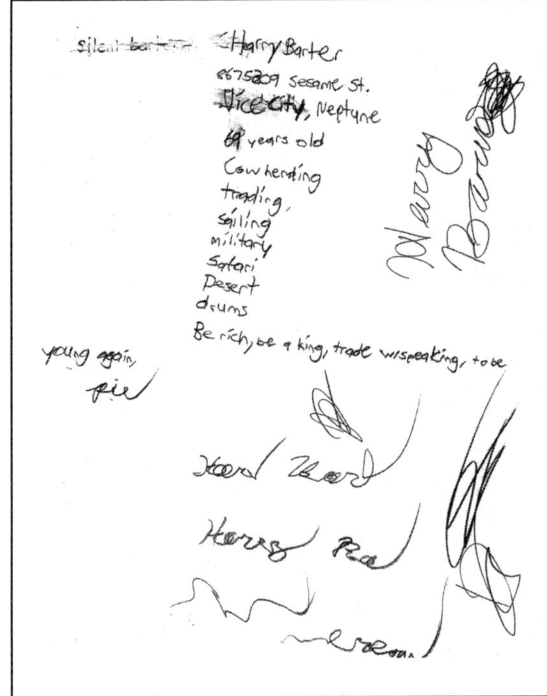

Harry Barter
8675309 Sesame St.
Vice City, Neptune
69 years old
Cow herding
trading,
sailing
military
Safari
Desert
drums
Be rich, be a king, trade wispeaking, to be
young again,
fire

Figure 3.4a *Harry* **Barter**'*s Prewrite Profile*

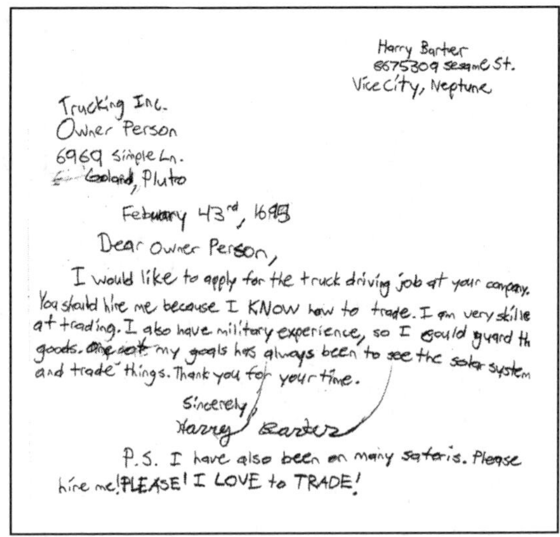

Harry Barter
8675309 Sesame St.
Vice City, Neptune

Trucking Inc.
Owner Person
6969 Simple Ln.
Gooland, Pluto

Febuary 43rd, 1699

Dear Owner Person,

I would like to apply for the truck driving job at your company. You should hire me because I KNOW how to trade. I am very skille at trading. I also have military experience, so I could guard th goods. my goals has always been to see the solar system and trade things. Thank you for your time.

Sincerely,
Harry Barter

P.S. I have also been on many safaris. Please hire me! PLEASE! I LOVE to TRADE!

Figure 3.4b *Harry* **Barter**'*s Business Letter*

job interviews during which the interviewee had to assume the persona of the vocabulary word, answering questions knowledgably. *Oasis* confessed that he liked to take a lot of breaks under palm trees and he was looking forward to a future as a resort. *Barter* bragged about her trading skills, and *Migration* just couldn't sit still. After each interview we discussed whether the interviewee (representing the vocabulary word) had provided a true representation of itself. Katie and Sherri reported that following that one class period of word study through business letters and job interviews, students were able to show understanding of the entire word list.

Writing Sequence Descriptions

Vocabulary One, Two, Three

Sequences provide us with the facts in perfect order. First, second, third. Sequences tell us how to bake the cookies, clean the cat box, and fight a forest fire. We gather our tools, our wits, our prior knowledge in reading directions, and tackle the unknown through steps one, two, three. From a writer's perspective, we are not trying to be artful, but to clearly take the reader step-by-step down a logical path in the most comprehensible way possible.

> ***Michael:*** As a former writer of work instructions for everything from metal-cutting screw machines to maintaining boilers with the capacity of taking out a city block, I can testify that comprehensibility lies in the orderly sequence of details.
>
> ***Sara:*** And I can bear witness that an incomprehensible sequence description might make an otherwise nonviolent person want to stab a Barbie Dream House with a screwdriver at 11:57 P.M. on Christmas Eve.

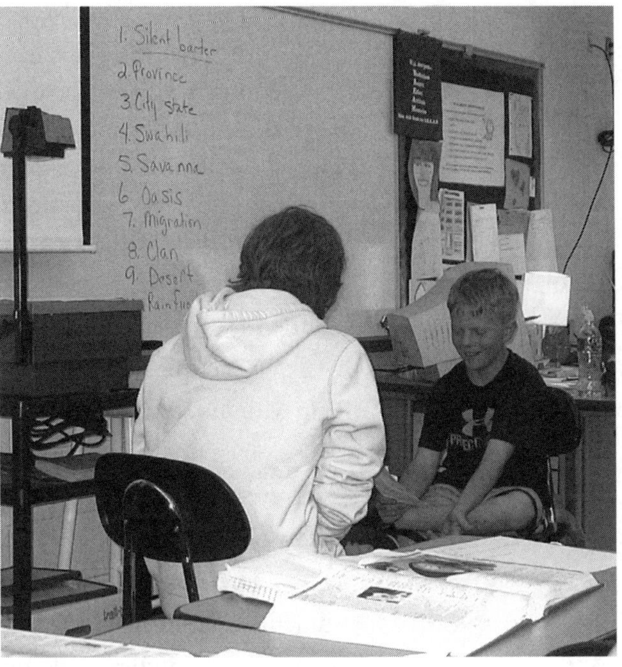

Figure 3.5 *Sixth graders interview a vocabulary word.*

Combining a lesson in writing sequences along with a vocabulary lesson is a logical, straightforward path to word mastery. Depending on the vocabulary word's part of speech (noun, verb, adverb, adjective) a writer can provide a sequenced route to understanding as to what that word is and/or how it behaves, motivating the student to make the word explain itself in a logical manner. In this sample, we see what steps lead ***miscalculate*** to reach a wrong answer. (See Appendix D for a copy of this sequence in a reproducible format.)

Miscalculate Sequence Description

In order to *miscalculate*, follow this seven-step plan:

1. Pick ten apples.
2. Put them in a basket and count them again.

3. Make sure you have exactly a total of ten apples.
4. Pick two more apples.
5. Put those two apples in the basket and recount.
6. Add all the apples for a new total.
7. Announce that you now have fifteen apples in the basket.

It's usually pretty easy to figure out how to *miscalculate*, as long as you know what the word means. But how about a word whose meaning is a little fuzzier; what are the steps to ***success*** for instance?

We have been fortunate in that we have had a continuing relationship with the students at Bay Middle School in Bay Village, Ohio. In the 2008/2009 school year, Katie Lufkin worked with her principal, Sean Andrews, to identify twenty-six sixth-grade students who were all working below benchmark. These students were grouped into one language arts class where Katie was joined by another teacher to address these students' special needs throughout the year. By spring we celebrated along with the students and teachers as the kids (now ALL working at benchmark level) prepared to take the Ohio Achievement Test (OAT). Everyone was looking for *success*. To help get the kids psyched and remind them of the elements of effective test taking, we wrote a sequence description together on the word *success*.

First we showed them two sequence descriptions. (See Appendix D, *miscalculate*, and Appendix E, ***meander***, for copies in a reproducible format.)

Meander Sequence Description

In order to *meander*, follow this simple six-step plan:

1. Go to step three.
2. Wander aimlessly in and out of every room humming nonsensical tunes, then proceed to step four.
3. Go to step two.
4. Investigate any object at the edge of one's peripheral vision but not for any length of time that exceeds thirty seconds.
5. Do not move in a straight line under any circumstances; feel free to circle back.
6. Repeat step one.

We discussed what these sequences had in common and asked the students if the sequence led them to understand the meanings of *miscalculate* and *meander*. We talked about places that we might come across sequence writing, which included instructions for games, recipes, rules, and even directions for taking a proficiency test. Since the upcoming test was on everyone's mind, we then discussed what it would take to attain *success* on the OAT. For our group write, the students chose to draft their sequences in the form of a recipe.

Assemble all ingredients
Pour in a bowl one ton of preparation
Add two teaspoons of complete sentences
Mix in a teaspoon of process of elimination
Add a gallon of rereading
Blend in a quart of main ideas
Shake with a dash of self-esteem
Whip in a sharpened #2 pencil
Add a ladle of details
Bake for 2.5 hours while checking it over
And then serve to your teacher

We adapted our prewrite a little for this exercise. We made three columns, one with measurement terms, one with verbs for cooking, and one with actions known to lead to *success* (see Figure 3.8). Using this brainstorm, we were quickly able to assemble our recipe. The students then wrote recipe definitions on their own, first engaging in collaborative discussion and then composing in their writer's notebooks. One student wrote a recipe for ***peace*** worthy of serving up in the kitchens of world leaders around the globe. Another took the *success* theme to a different, more musical level and wrote a recipe for the *success* of the school's band director. In the students' notebooks, you can also see the warm-up exercise in which the writer defined the word ***ferocious*** in a poem (see Chapter 7, "Writing Poetry"). Both the recipe sequence and the warm-up poem were completed in one fifty-minute classroom period.

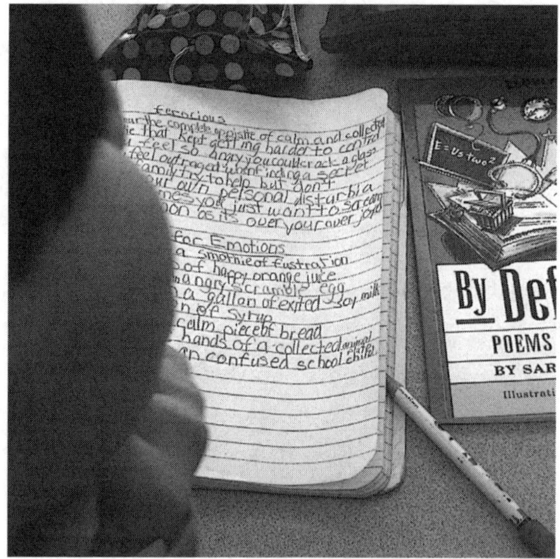

Figure 3.6 *Recipe for* **Emotions**

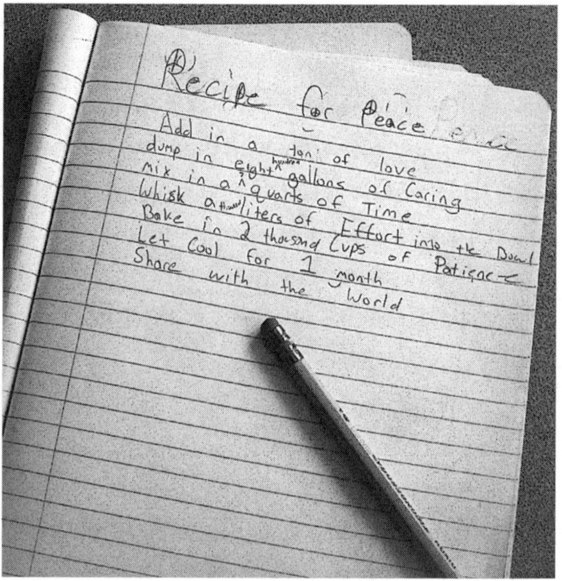

Figure 3.7 *Recipe for* **Peace**

Writing an Obituary

Dead but Not Buried

Type "Death becomes you" into your search engine and you turn up everything from Broadway musicals to movies, reality shows, blogs, and lyrics by 50 Cent.

> ***Michael:*** Did you see the one about how they had the aspiring top models pose in their own death scenes for that reality show?
>
> ***Sara:*** No, thanks. I'll pass. Who would watch that?
>
> ***Michael:*** Apparently the reality show's audience demographic.
>
> ***Sara:*** Wouldn't that demographic be similar to the one to whom we are pitching our vocabulary lessons?
>
> ***Michael:*** Bingo.

When we first suggested this exercise to teacher Carol Reinhardt, who teaches at an alternative high school in Iowa, she replied, "My kids are just twisted enough to really get into this one." And they did. In fact, kids from grades 6 and up were excited to knock off one word after another for the opportunity to write the biographical obituary reports. First we had to take a minute and define the word ***obituary***. Samples, of course, can be found in newspapers and online. We have also provided two fictional word obituaries in Appendices F and G.

> ***Michael:*** According to the link provided at www.cremation.com . . .
>
> ***Sara:*** Seriously. That's a real website?
>
> ***Michael:*** Deadly serious, and it has lots of samples, too.

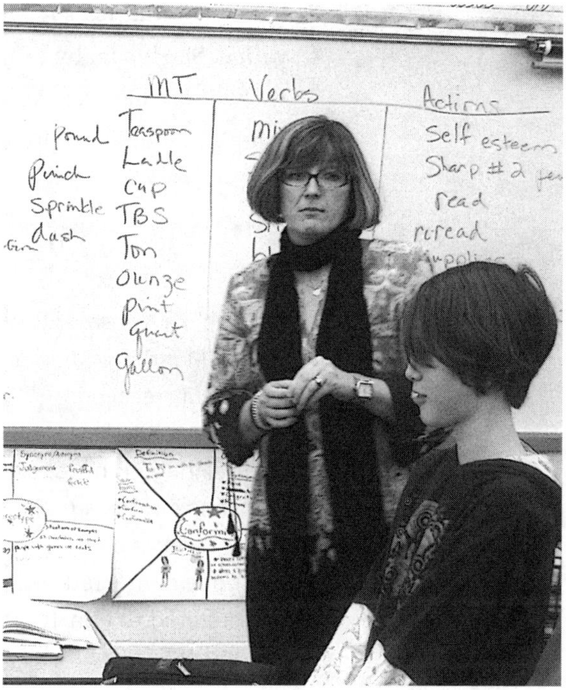

Figure 3.8 *Katie Lufkin in Her Sixth-Grade Classroom*

Anyway, according to these experts, an obituary "can be as basic as containing only public facts about a person's life. Their birth, family tree, their death," or "It can also be a very personal look at a life. Not only a summation of the public facts, but a glimpse of the uniqueness; that, when combined with those 'facts,' creates a personality" (Cremation.com 2009).

Defining a personality and life history for a word requires really getting to know that word, how it lived and then, alas, what led to its demise. At Bay Middle School, the unknown words for the obituary writing had arisen during the students' fervent free reading of fantasy fiction. This list of words prepared to shake off their mortal coils included: ***voracious***, ***timorous***, ***bondage***, ***aggrieved***, ***corrupt***, and ***brazen***. The phrase "Mrs. Lufkin, what's this word mean?" had motivated Katie to keep a running list of the words she had been called on to define.

We had been in Katie's classroom several times that school year writing business letters, poems, diary entries, and other genres of writing. So when we suggested to Katie that we might like to see what kids could do with obituaries, she put our model lesson into action and the kids ran with it. She began by projecting one of the sample vocabulary obituaries we had sent her (see Appendix F, ***insipid***, and Appendix G, ***convivial***, for samples suitable for projection).

Sample Obituary for *Insipid*

Topeka, Kansas (AP)—*Insipid*, a rather bland adjective, passed away on Monday of unknown causes. The age of the deceased was not readily recalled.

It is believed that *Insipid* may have died of boredom while painting his house beige. Passersby did not notice him until Thursday because he blended into his surroundings unremarkably.

Insipid's career as a doorstop spanned several decades yet none contacted could recall any achievements that could be credited to him. It seems *Insipid*'s life was marked by not standing out.

When asked to comment on *Insipid's* life, surviving brother (and polar opposite), Spicy, replied, "I had a brother?"

Insipid is also survived by his wife, Boring; twin daughters Tasteless and Soporific; and his son, Vapid.

In lieu of memorial services the family chose to watch grass grow.

Sample Obituary for *Convivial*

New Orleans, LA (*Party Time Magazine*)—*Convivial*, a very social adjective, died Saturday night surrounded by friends. *Convivial* passed away while dancing on a tabletop, wearing a lampshade on her head and singing "Let's Get This Party Started."

Convivial's life was punctuated by one festive gathering after another. She was known as the life of the party, leading parades and making friends wherever she went. *Convivial* was elected the *most fun to be around* by her high school graduating class and lived up to that reputation.

Next-door neighbor Reticent said upon *Convivial*'s passing, "Finally we might get some peace and quiet in this building!

Hopefully someone less social will move in now."

Memorial services for *Convivial* will be held in the grand ballroom of Caesar's Palace in Las Vegas starting on Thursday and are expected to continue for the next seven months.

Savanah Georgia

Voracious, a greedy adjective died yesterday of obeisity Voracious spent his life eating Big Macs at McDonalds, stuffing himself. His friend satisfied said "I knew someday he would just POP!" Voracious is surived by his wife Piggish, his son egear, and his daughter avid.

Figure 3.9 *Obituary for* **Voracious**

The class discussed the qualities of the death notices and then broke into small groups of three and four. They used the prewrite Collaboration Cheat Sheet (Appendix A) along with dictionaries, thesauruses, and some of the context clues in several different fantasy novels. In the spirit of killing multiple classroom goals with one assignment, she challenged each writing group to use at least one quote in every definition obituary (proper punctuation required). Finally, the obituaries were shared aloud, with appropriate solemnities and condolences.

Figure 3.10 *Obituary for* **Timorous**

HongKong China

Timorous a shy adjective died yesterday by being afraid of a roller coaster and Falling off. Fearless the chipmuck "Said he was a big baby since he didn't do anything daring." Timorous surived by his brother Timid the hippo and his shy mom the Koloa.

Figure 3.11 *Obituary for* **Brazen**

Jacksonville, Florida

Brazen, a shameless adjictive who died yesterday, assumed he wouldn't get caught for murder. Brazen spent his life being over conifident.

His friend dissgraceful said "He would always be prasumpuious about what he did" He is Surrivied by his wife impudent and his son shameless.

Michael: Sneaky of Katie to slip in a little grammar lesson.

Sara: Love it. Hope our readers take this as a cue to adapt these lessons to their classroom needs.

Composing an Interview

"Where Do You See Yourself a Year from Now?"

What would a word like ***competitive*** like to see happen? Where does ***regress*** see itself in five years? What are ***malevolent***'s major strengths, and has it ever committed a felony?

Michael: That would depend on what the interviewer means by the word *it*.

Sara: Nice try. Interviewers strive to reveal who the interviewees really are.

Michael: That would depend on what you mean by *are*.

Sara: Can we move on here?

Just as if you were to stage an interview with Rosa Parks or Piggy from *Lord of the Flies* in order to further students' knowledge of a historical or fictional character, preparing for an interview with a vocabulary word requires preparation on the part of both the interviewer and the interviewee, enabling a conversation.

Interviews are most often done live. Even of those relegated to print, many are transcriptions of face-to-face exchanges. From job interviews to red carpet assaults, the key to interviewing success is having adequate background knowledge. From our perspective, interviews are not only good for the participants, but also perfect for classroom performance.

Back in Katie Lufkin's and Sherri Deal's sixth-grade social studies classrooms, students composed job interviews with words about the Sahara Desert (a natural progression having previously written cover letters for job applications for vocabulary words). We began by having two students read the following interview aloud and followed up with a discussion of what makes a good interview. The key to getting the interviewee to talk, we determined, was to ask questions that could not be answered with a simple yes or no. We wanted questions that would give us insight into the interviewee. (See Appendix H for a sample interview suitable for projection.)

Sample Interview for *Malevolent*

Malevolent applies for a position at a fast-food restaurant.

Q *What qualifies you for this position?*
A Well, first of all, I would have no problem selling unhealthy food to anyone. In fact, I would hope that anyone who came to the restaurant would end up sick. I could serve food past its expiration date without thinking twice—actually I would rather sell food that is rotten so I could help get rid of old inventory.

Q *What is your experience?*
A I really don't like people all that much so I think I would fit in well as counter help. I've become good at ignoring the needs of others by being mean to my little brother and I know I could carry this experience into my job here.

Q *What have you done to prepare you for this job?*
A I have served cereal to my little brother with spoiled milk and it didn't bother me at all when he blew chunks afterward. I even did it twice.

Q *What are your goals?*
A I just want to get my way—I really don't care if anyone gets hurt feelings because of my actions. Sometimes it's just more rewarding to see someone cry. I guess one of my goals is to make people feel really bad. I think I would find selling greasy food really rewarding.

Q *What are your strengths?*
A I don't let other people's feelings get in my way.

Q *What are your weaknesses?*
A I don't think I have any.

After the class discussed the quality and content of the questions, we talked about different instances where we have seen interviews (TV news, red carpets, MTV, cop shows). The interviewers and interviewees then collaborated, first on paper and then in performance, easily meeting the challenge to ask and answer at least six questions about each word. We began by asking the whole class to think up questions we might want to ask the word *oasis* as part of our Collaboration Cheat Sheet and group write. We didn't even bother to answer the questions in our modeling, kids were too anxious to work on their own interviews.

First, the groups completed their own Cheat Sheets, and then crafted their interviews as a group. This classroom sample, an interview of Joe and Julie ***Clan*** (aka Rachel and Sara) by James, Ashley, and Kendall, was actually composed by all five participants. Joe and Julie *Clan* are being interviewed for jobs as teachers (see Figure 3.12). They feel they are qualified because they would be able to lead a *clan* of students. The performance was well scripted, with everyone taking a part and everyone getting to ask or answer at least one question. In our follow-up discussion we asked, "So what's the difference between a *clan* and a ***mob***?" Another student who was not part of this writing group offered that members of a *clan* claim to be descendents of a common ancestor. Everyone agreed that a final version of their interview should contain some questions about Joe and Julie *Clan*'s roots.

Figure 3.12 *Jo and Julie* **Clan** *Interview*

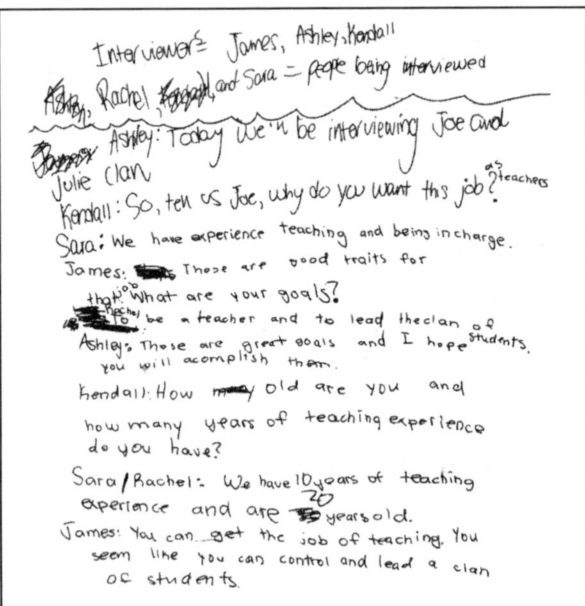

Interviewers: James, Ashley, Kendall
Rachel, and Sara = people being interviewed
Ashley: Today we'll be interviewing Joe and Julie clan
Kendall: So, tell us Joe, why do you want this job? as teachers
Sara: We have experience teaching and being in charge.
James: Those are good traits for that. What are your goals?
To be a teacher and to lead the clan of students.
Ashley: Those are great goals and I hope you will acomplish them.
Kendall: How old are you and how many years of teaching experience do you have?
Sara/Rachel: We have 10 years of teaching experience and are 20 years old.
James: You can get the job of teaching. You seem like you can control and lead a clan of students.

The students did not go on to rewrite this interview. After all, we were in a social studies classroom and the important goal of the lesson from Katie's and Sherri's perspectives was that all students would gain an understanding of the word. Through collaboration, research, writing, and discussion, we had met that goal while building on the student's knowledge of interviewing techniques. While debriefing after the lesson, Katie and Sherri were quick to say that learning how to conduct an interview would be very useful in future lessons as they frequently approached historical events as if they were current events and confirmed that interviews can and do happen in a social studies classroom.

Tier One: Basic Words

Easier	Harder
random	rookery
certain	symmetry
chance	metamorphosis
ecosystem	organism
oasis	heritage
barter	haggle
emperor	protectorate
habitat	satellite
trek	encampment
clan	sanctuary

Tier Two: Conceptual Words

Easier	Harder
vicious	sadistic
precious	venomous
vanish	evaporate
distressed	aggrieved
experimental	probationary
apprehensive	timorous
voracious	insatiable
nomad	itinerant
intolerant	myopic
obsessive	relentless
brazen	audacious

Lesson Process

❶ **Share** samples of the explanatory writing genre with your students by reading it out loud and or projecting it. You may use our samples from the appendices or you may decide to choose other models. For example, you may feel it more practical to introduce a news story or an obituary by reading one aloud from the local paper to familiarize your students with the form. There may be business and friendly letters in your social studies textbook that you may wish to share as samples (Martin Luther King, Jr.'s letter from Birmingham jail, for instance).

❷ **Discuss** the qualities of explanatory writing with the class. How does the formality of a business letter compare with casualness of a friendly email? What kinds of words are used when writing directions that need to follow a certain sequence for the task being described to be successful? Why is order important? Discuss particular structures or patterns utilized when writing in the explanatory genre. For example, the question and answer format in an interview, the heading and closing of a letter, or the information that is integral to an obituary: date of birth, occupation, surviving family members, and so on.

❸ **Model** the process by co-creating one of these word-pieces along with your students, with you scribing their suggestions on the board or projector starting with the Collaboration Cheat Sheet. If you decide to add an extra step—as we did with the business letter by creating extra details that would come in handy for a job applicant—make sure you model this as well. Leave all these examples on the board while students are working on their own pieces.

❹ **Choose and collaborate.** Choose or assign vocabulary words (see Chapter 2, "Choosing the Words") for your writers or groups of writers. The number of words you assign for each group of collaborators will depend on the type of explanatory writing the class is doing. Simple step-by-step directions will not be as time-consuming as a resume cover letter, for example. You may decide to assign one word per student in the case of the longer pieces, but allow them to collaborate with each other on all the words assigned to the working group during the brainstorming sessions. This way the students still receive the benefit of the small-group discussion but are not overwhelmed with the production of artifacts of their learning.

❺ **Provide** vocabulary research materials for your students. Take a look back at our ideas about Researching Words in the Digital Age (on page xi). Encourage the students to include any secondary meanings that they have discovered for their words. As always, double-check words provided by the thesaurus against another source for meaning. Newspapers, magazines, cookbooks, even assembly instructions for a home entertainment unit can be the source of mentor texts for the explanatory genre. Nothing makes a lesson seem more genuine for students than real-world examples.

❻ **Write.** Provide time for the students to write their explanatory pieces. A good rule of thumb is to provide equal brainstorming and writing session times. But we are by no means suggesting the implementation of a stopwatch. We want students to get their work down in Version 1; we can always go back later and tighten up the text. Students may decide to write their pieces collaboratively within their small groups or may decide to write on their own. Either will work; we have found the most important collaboration occurs during the brainstorming sessions as the Collaboration Cheat Sheet is developed.

❼ **Turn and talk.** Have students share their writing out loud with someone near them. No fair just passing the paper to another student to read. We want the reader to experience their words as they say them out loud.

> ***Michael:*** Ostensibly one might think that explanatory writing is not often read out loud but we beg to differ.
>
> ***Sara:*** How many times have you been composing an important letter and turned to someone you trust, asking, "How does this sound?"
>
> ***Michael:*** Or what about step-by-step instructions from that exotically accented tech support person on the other end of the phone line?

❽ **Perform.** Invite students to present their word-pieces to the whole class. We decided to present our business letters as part of a job interview with the rest of the class playing the part of "fly on the wall." If students have written step-by-step instructions you may have one student read the directions while others assist by acting out those guidelines. Obituaries could be presented at a lectern as eulogies, dropping the words into an urn after they have been put to rest.

❾ **Assess.** Lead the class in a discussion of the writing and performance they have just experienced. Ask the students what they think the new vocabulary word means and what it doesn't mean. Just as important, could the students hear and understand the performance? Don't be shy about having the performers repeat their presentation, since doing so will not only improve the presenters' fluency but the repetition will reinforce the vocabulary lesson.

10 **Hazards.** Explanatory writing relies on following a specific pattern whether it is a set of assembly instructions or the order of mixing ingredients in a recipe. Students may need to be reminded to include all steps necessary. It may help to suggest to them that their reader knows absolutely nothing about the subject matter that they are presenting and not to assume any prior knowledge on their audience's part.

11 **Extra credit.** This genre lends itself to the creation of product manuals. A handbook or instruction guide for the vocabulary words from Lois Lowry's *The Giver*, for example, could be compiled of the step-by-step sequences written by the students. A newspaper obituary page laid out with headlines and photos is another fun activity. Students could write replies to the business letters deepening their understanding of the vocabulary through further interactions.

High Definition Through Persuasive Writing

Do you have trouble getting your students to do what you think is in their best interest?

Are your instructions ignored or followed poorly?

Are you at your wit's end?

Well, vigorous vocabulary instructions can help—just follow these five easy steps to successful teaching—guaranteed to work every time or double your money back!

You can't flip on the news or pick up a bottle of milk without someone trying to persuade you to TRY THIS! DON'T MISS! Or perhaps the scariest, TAKE THIS, YOU'LL FEEL BETTER! Persuasive writing is everywhere, complete with real and implied explanation points urging you to ACT NOW! The messages are so omnipresent that we may fool ourselves into thinking that we are no longer even receptive to the pleas, but we are. And the best way to understand how persuasive argument works is to build one using new vocabulary words.

Whether in the form of an opinion editorial (op-ed), a persuasive speech, an advertisement, a bumper sticker, a propaganda poster, or an infomercial, persuasive writing describes a situation and then attempts to convince the audience to "come on down" and adopt the writer's point of view. Since we all have opinions, this genre of writing has a natural appeal for student writers. Simply pointing out to kids that persuasive writing can help them build a strong argument for the next time they want a video game or curfew adjustment could be enough to convince them to tune in.

For or against, the student writer chooses a stand and then utilizes specifics and logic to convince and sway the audience. While crafting a persuasive argument might appear to come to kids as naturally as sibling rivalry, there are some things we can do to help motivate students to compose effective arguments. Standard topics for students include taking a stand for or against the death penalty, the Electoral College, or vaccinations—topics in which kids may not have a here-and-now vested interest. And one thing we know about kids is that they are all about the here and now. According to teachers Richard Beach and Candance Doerr-Stevens, "Students are often not invested in writing about an issue because they assume that they have no agency to affect change, so, why bother. If they sense that voicing their opinions may lead to change, they may then be motivated to formulate effective arguments for their positions, as well as propose possible solutions" (Beach and Doerr-Stevens 2009).

Providing students with an opportunity to showcase their persuasive arguments through an endgame, classroom performance can in and of itself be a motivating factor, the prospective audience providing an authentic reason for students to create and polish their persuasions. Combining persuasive writing with vocabulary study is a particularly effective learning activity since word choice is of paramount importance. Think of the age-old ploy of burning dirty coal's having been labeled a Clean Air Initiative and you begin to see that corporate persuaders think long and hard about word choice. And you can bet that thinking was done in conjunction with coal cars of collaboration. In fact, talking through our arguments is a way of test-driving ideas before committing them to paper to see which are strongest.

Sara: I remember listening to my daughter, who, at about age three, was trying to persuade a neighborhood boy to play house when he wanted to play football.

Michael: Tough sell?

Sara: He didn't want anything to do with her new kitchen set or playing house. After a few rounds of argument, she capitulated. "Okay," she said, "We'll play football. You be the Daddy and I'll be the Mommy."

Michael: Ah, the old changing the rules while the ball's in the air trick, but not exactly what we would call a well-crafted persuasive argument.

Changing the rules, repeating the same line over and over and over and over until its meaning is lost, whining, chest bumping, and the ultimate my-way-or-the-highway kind of threat—these are the forms of persuasion that kids are accustomed to seeing in the media. In TV and movie fantasyland, they work! Of course, on TV there are always conveniently open parking places wherever the hero is going and women in high heels can outrun a bomb blast. This imperfect logic based on shallow emotional appeals may hold sway over the typical television viewer consciously suspending his disbelief, but these shallow lines of attack won't go very far in the real world.

"While emotional appeals can certainly influence people's beliefs, students also need to know how to use factual evidence and counter-arguments to influence beliefs," Beach and Doerr-Stevens tell us (2009). To craft an argument that the reader doesn't want to refuse, you must show that the facts are on your side. As educational psychologist May Li writes, "Persuasion is generally an exercise in creating a win-win situation. You present a case that others find beneficial to agree with" (2008). She lays out ten techniques to help writers make their cases more compelling, which we have adapted to suit the needs of the middle school classroom.

1. **Repetition.** Talk to anyone well versed in learning psychology, and they'll tell you repetition is crucial. It's also critical in persuasive writing, since a person can't agree with you if they don't truly get what you're saying. Of course, there's good repetition and bad. To stay on the good side, make your point in several different ways, such as stating it directly, using an example, finding it in a story or via a quote from a famous person, and stating it once more in your summary.

2. **Reasons Why.** Remember the power of the word ***because***. Psychological studies have shown that people are more likely to comply with a request if you simply give them a reason why, even if that reason makes no sense. The strategy itself does make sense if you think about it. We don't like to be told things or asked to take action without a reasonable explanation. When you need people to be receptive to your line of thinking, always give reasons why.

3. **Consistency.** It's been called the "hobgoblin of little minds," but consistency in our thoughts and actions is a valued social trait. We don't want to appear inconsistent, since, whether fair or not, that characteristic is associated with instability and flightiness, while consistency is associated with integrity and rational behavior.

Use this in your writing by getting the reader to agree with something up front that most people would have a hard time disagreeing with. Then rigorously make your case, with plenty of supporting evidence, all while relating your ultimate point back to the opening scenario that's already been accepted.

4. **Social Proof.** Looking for guidance from others as to what to do and what to accept is one of the most powerful psychological forces in our lives. Obvious examples of social proof can be found in testimonials and outside referrals, and it's the driving force behind social media.

5. **Comparisons.** Metaphors, similes, and analogies are the persuasive writer's best friends. When you can relate your scenario to

something that the reader already accepts as true, you're well on your way to convincing someone to see things your way. But comparisons work in other ways, too. Sometimes you can be more persuasive by comparing apples to oranges.

6. Agitate and Solve. This is a persuasion theme that works as an overall approach to making your case. First, you identify the problem and qualify your audience. Then you agitate the reader's pain before offering your solution as the answer that will make it all better.

The agitation phase is not about being sadistic; it's about empathy. You want the reader to know unequivocally that you understand his problem because you've dealt with it and/or are experienced at eliminating it. The credibility of your solution goes way up if you demonstrate that you truly feel the prospect's pain.

7. Prognosticate. Another persuasion theme involves providing your readers with a glimpse into the future. Use images and detailed descriptions to herald exactly how this product or campaign will change the reader's life, make the world fall in love with them, and bring them riches beyond their wildest dreams. This entire strategy is built on credibility. If you have no idea what you're talking about, you'll end up looking foolish. But if you can back up your claims with your credentials or your obvious grasp of the subject matter, this is an extremely persuasive technique.

8. Go Tribal. Despite our attempts to be sophisticated, evolved beings, we humans are exclusionary by nature. Give someone a chance to be a part of a group that they want to be in—whether that be wealthy, hip, green, or even contrarian—and they'll hop on board whatever train you're driving. Find out what group your audience wants to be in, and offer them an invitation to join your seemingly exclusive and desirable group.

9. Address Objections. Address all the potential objections of at least the majority of your readers. If you really know your subject, the arguments against you should be fairly obvious. A huge part of the writer's job is to anticipate the "yes-buts" and refute them before they can knock you off your soapbox and undercut your argument.

10. Storytelling. Storytelling is really a catchall technique—you can and should use it in combination with any and all of the previous nine strategies. But the reason why storytelling works so well lies at the heart of what persuasion really is. Stories allow people to persuade themselves, and that's what it's really all about. You might say that we never convince anyone of anything, we simply help others independently decide that we're right. Do everything you can to tell better stories, and you'll find that you are a terribly persuasive person. (Li 2008)

May Li's insights are compatible with the NCTE/IRA guidelines for persuasive argument: statement of thesis, three main reasons, three facts or examples supporting each reason, and conclusion. However, those guidelines are really more about structure than content—a vessel without the juice. The author tells us what to put in the vessel to persuade others to drink up.

Michael: Is this some kind of Kool-Aid metaphor? Because if it is, I want some more details. Flavor? Color? Sweetness? Will it help me run faster, jump higher?

Sara: That's just the kind of descriptive detail we need to win over our audience.

Writing Well-Crafted Argument

He Said, She Said

In order to construct an effective persuasive argument we need to be good storytellers (see Chapter 5, "Narrative Writing"). We must understand our subject from more than one point of view. We need to relate to our audience members and position ourselves as being able to meet their needs. Showing students the methods advertisers and others use when trying to persuade us, from repetition to storytelling testimonials, will not only help them in their own writing, but also help them to think more critically about, and perhaps even resist, what they see in the media.

One book that we like to use to introduce the concept of persuasion and the techniques people use is the children's picture book, *Don't Let the Pigeon Drive the Bus!* by Mo Willems (2003) (for kids of all ages). In the book, Pigeon begs, manipulates, bribes, and finally throws a bonkers tantrum trying to wheedle his way into the driver's seat, without success. This book provides any number of opportunities to discuss effective and ineffective persuasive methods. According to NCTE and IRA guidelines, this skill cannot be taught too early.

> ***Michael:*** Good advice. Advertisers get busy trying to persuade toddlers to crave cheesy plastic toys and fast food.
>
> ***Sara:*** Too true. And the best way to recognize when you are trying to be persuaded is to learn how arguments are crafted.

In a November 2009 interview on CNN, Google CEO Eric Schmidt observed that as a child his education often consisted of memorizing facts, a system that is now outdated since all facts are readily available through (what else?) Google. Instead, he suggested, we must be teaching students how to ask the right questions and sort through the masses of burgeoning data available on computers (which double in power every eighteen months) to find answers. Since entities from politicians to corporations want to control their public image, there is a lot of spin on information available on the Internet—much of it patently false. He further advised that since information is now available without screening by editorial gatekeepers, what students really need to be learning is how to unravel the persuasive and pervasive bias to find the truth.

With that in mind, we set out to persuade students to build better vocabularies by spinning their own web of advertisements. We started with the least subtle and most fun model: the infomercial.

Developing an Infomercial

But That's Not All!

In order to find mentor text for developing an infomercial and not get bogged down by all those *Law and Order* reruns on television, we turned to the Internet. YouTube is a ready resource to tap into to introduce persuasive writing. Type in the word ***infomercial*** and you will find over 24,000 examples—1,300 just for pitchman Billy Mays and parodies thereof. We downloaded one of Mays' diatribes for an odor eliminator, a product called What Odor?™ to introduce the concept while working in Christine Landaker-Charbonneau's eighth-grade language arts class at Pierce Middle School in Milton, Massachusetts.

Sara: Whether it was the imagined whiff of a foul odor or the shared experience of infomercials, that video clip really got things going.

Michael: After showing the clip, we parsed the pitch to see if it had a pattern we could follow in our own writing. We noticed that the pitchman began with a question introducing a problem that needed solving.

Sara: Then you showed them the infomercial that you had written (see Appendix I for a projectable sample).

Figure 4.1 *What Order?™ Infomercial*

Sample Infomercial for Enthusiam

Are you tired of being tired? Perplexed over being pooped? Fed up with fatigue?!

Hi!!! Millie Bays here and I want to introduce to you a brand-new product that will change your life—*ENTHUSIASM!* No more dragging your feet around the house or office annoying your friends, family, and coworkers. Just half a cup of *ENTHUSIASM* is all you need to turn the most mundane task into an enjoyable adventure because *ENTHUSIASM* is not just a product, *it's a way of life. ENTHUSIASM* gives you the get-up-and-go, sure, but that's not all. *ENTHUSIASM* includes the secret ingredient *INTEREST*, which keeps your energy and concentration at peak performance level.

Watch as others around you become discouraged and give up—BUT NOT YOU! Because you had the keen insight to employ this amazing new product, *ENTHUSIASM*! Even the most common, humdrum tasks such as cleaning the cat's litter box, loading the dishwasher, or scrubbing the bathroom tiles become a pleasure when *ENTHUSIASM* is employed. ACT NOW and we will include *ENTHUSIASM*'s companion product, FERVOR, at absolutely no extra charge (you pay only for shipping and handling).

This is Millie Bays asking you to get yourself some *ENTHUSIASM*! (Product may not be effective in some institutions of higher learning or dentist's offices.)

Sara: You read the text aloud with just the right expression to mimic the hawkers on TV.

Michael: With ***enthusiasm***?

Figure 4.2 *Michael Modeling the Collaboration Cheat Sheet*

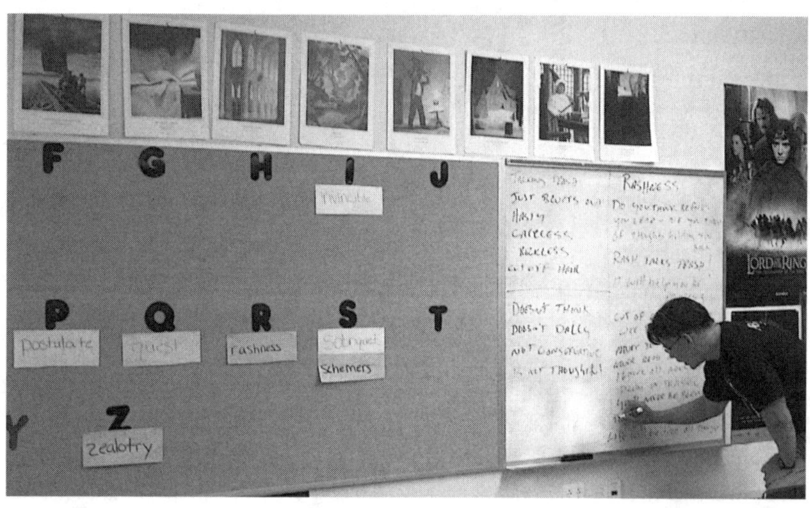

Sara: You might say that. The kids certainly made an immediate connection.

Michael: First, I asked for someone to choose a word from the word wall for our group write, and they chose ***rashness***. With one scholar helping with a dictionary and another with a thesaurus, we first completed the prewrite Collaboration Cheat Sheet (see Figure 4.3) and then drafted our pitch.

Sara: When you led the class in a group write, you could barely keep up! Ideas were flying from the kids.

Christine's is an inclusion class, so following the group write, we also teamed with special education teacher Kelli Prodanas to help the students break into small groups and select a word from the word wall in the back of the classroom for further study. Among the choices were ***aquatic***, ***invincible***, ***quest***, ***zealotry***, ***sobriquet***, ***don***, ***demeanor***, ***evangelism***, ***schemers***, and ***rashness***, all words from recent classroom readings. The students collaborated, using dictionaries and thesauruses to complete the Collaboration Cheat Sheet (Appendix A). As with all classes, after researching and conferring about the word meaning, some students chose to write in groups and a few wrote independently. Immediately, students began drafting, inserting product warnings and admonitions that buyers had to be age fourteen or older to order—details based on their real-world experience with infomercials. Each followed the model and began with a question and the implication that this word would provide answers:

Figure 4.3 *Prewrite Collaboration Cheat Sheet*

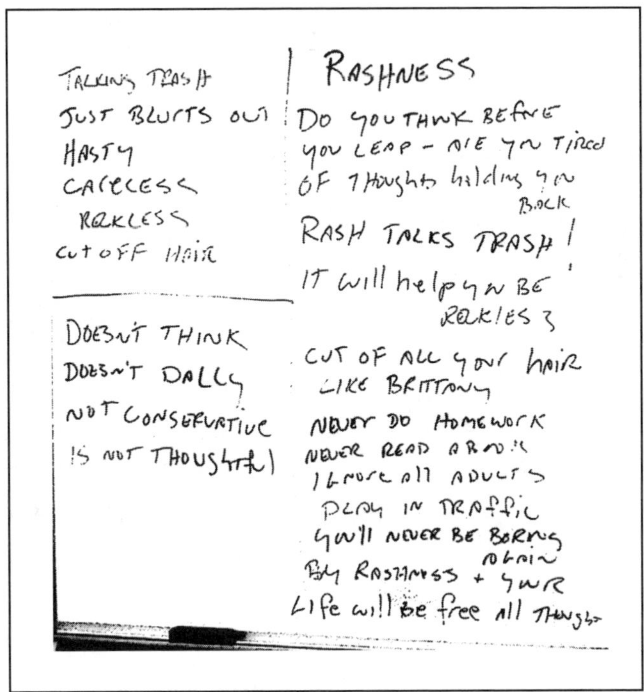

> Tired of thinking before speaking? Want to eat everything off the dinner table? Buy *Rashness.*

> Do you like going on adventures but can't find one? Then you need to buy some *Quest.*

Invincible

Not capable of being conqured or over come, unconqureable
can't be defeated
irresistible, unconquerable
an adult
Superhero (to fly pick up car move through traffic)

defeatable
child
Human

~~Are you eshamed of not have super powers? Well get them now. Become Invincible is now avaliable.~~

Are you tried of bullyies picking on you? Well get invinc-ible now.
Hi I'm Jhery Mesidor and I am selling Invinciable. If you don't want to die or ever be defeated by anyone get invincible.
If you Are afraid of getting mugged on a Street corner get invincible. wanna be The best hockey Player get invincible now at Shaws or Rite Aid but for The cheapest price call 1800 266 2981
sideeffects - cocky and hot temper.

Figure 4.4 **Invincible** *Infomercial with a Clever Disclaimer*

Are you tired of people calling you jellyfish, small, or SpongeBob? Do you wanna be hard, buff, and tough? What you need is *Invincible*. You can be just like Batman.

Coupling persuasive writing with word study is particularly useful because it causes students to look at the nuanced meanings of words. Employing the tools of secret ingredients and side effects leads to more fun and deeper thinking, and who can argue against that? Also in Christine's curriculum that week was an article about bullying. One student, Alex, wove their recent discussions about that article into his vocabulary infomercial, writing that being ***invincible*** makes you untouchable when it comes to bullying, an observation that was part not only of that week's lesson, but undoubtedly also of his daily experience.

Unfortunately, we had to return to Cleveland and were not present for the final performance of the word infomercials. Christine wrote to us to say that they had a blast with the final performances and that the kids did a great job with everyone being involved.

Whether writing an infomercial for *Enthusiasm* or an editorial signed by *Exclusivity*, students will develop a deeper understanding of new words through crafting a persuasive argument.

Sara: Remind students: don't forget the "ask."

Michael: Excuse me?

> ***Sara:*** I used to work for a nonprofit, the local chapter of the National Council on Alcohol and Drug Abuse, a United Way Agency. We would send out letters soliciting donations, trying to persuade potential donors to give money to middle-aged, recovering alcoholics. Given that our competition for donor dollars included adorable kids in wheelchairs, it was a tough sell. Sometimes we would get so caught up in our arguments and anecdotal stories, we would forget to ask for the money! Don't forget the "ask"!

Sobriquet

what it is: nickname
describes your personality, interest (adjective)
can: hurt peoples feelings

Its not: your full name, not your family name
can't: it can't be your actual name.

Are you [illegible] by your plain old name? Are you embarressed by your first name? Hi, I'm Kristina Tielo Binda and I'm hear to help you do something daring, get a Sobriquet! No more Lamey boring and embaressing names! Sobriquet can give you a reputation that you will love. A Sobriquet will make you cool. All of this is worth 18.99 but we will give you it for small fee of 5 dollars. Call now and we will double your offer. All you have to do is dial 617-750-3232, only pay shipping and handling.

Figure 4.5 *A* **sobriquet** *will make you cool!*

Studying persuasive writing invites students to read between the lines—to question the motivations of the author and to examine the techniques and patterns used to put forth a convincing line of reasoning. Encourage students to study several examples of persuasive mentor texts with a critical eye before attempting to write a piece of their own. We have provided a few projectable samples in the appendices you may wish to use for your read-alouds, but don't stop there. Examples of persuasive writing are easy resources for your students to research.

Writing Editorials and Persuasive Speeches

It's Only My Opinion, But . . .

In our sample opinion editorial (op-ed), ***Exclusivity*** (a librarian) advocates for a new rule barring ordinary citizens, particularly kids who might have sticky hands, from touching the books on her shelf (see Appendix J for a projectable sample).

Sample Op-Ed for *Exclusivity*

Open access to the library wastes money because it leads to the abuse of the books. Books are precious and they should not be allowed to circulate among the unwashed hands of mere students. Books need to be held for the *exclusive* benefit of teachers and librarians.

Restricted access to books will save money for the community. Worn books are worthless and allowing open library access wastes money and leads to tattered pages. Replacing lost or damaged books is very costly. When books are removed from the shelves, they must be put back, which increases work for librarians.

We must remove the word *public* from all libraries. Children particularly should be *excluded* from the library. They flip pages too fast and sometimes have food on their fingers. Last year students checked out books more than 800,000 times. Books were shared, toted in book bags, stashed in lockers, and taken home. This type of unrestricted use is dangerous for our books.

We must stop sharing books! Books should be for the *exclusive* use of teachers and librarians. Save money for our town and join me in restricting the free circulation of library books to just anyone.

Sincerely,
Exclusivity

After reading this aloud to your students, begin discussing by finding the synonyms and antonyms for the word. Who might be the intended audience for this op-ed? What are the reasons *Exclusivity* gives for not wanting to open the library to the public? What does *Exclusivity* ask for? After sharing this op-ed, you might wish to ask students to find op-eds in a local newspaper or magazine or download "in my opinion" pieces off of the Internet. Then follow the steps in the lesson process at the end of the chapter to guide students in creating their own vocabulary op-eds.

A persuasive speech, whether advocating for political office or a party invitation, is another form of persuasive writing. In the following mentor text ***Helium*** (projectable sample, Appendix K) asks to be invited to a party by proclaiming its strengths (makes balloons fly) and also addresses naysayers who claim that the chemical element does not play well with others.

Persuasive Oration for *Helium*

I am *Helium* and you should invite me to your party because I know how to keep things light. You may have heard that I do not play well with others. And that is true. I don't combine with my fellow chemicals at all. Instead I like to sneak around, odorless, colorless, some would say I am tasteless too, but I'm very entertaining. Most of those other chemicals smell like they never took a bath and they are simply TOO dense for me.

I hold myself apart, proud to be number two in the universe, knowing I am less dense than all the others (except for Hydrogen, who is so full of itself about being number one).

Don't hang with H! I never would.

I am popular, too! You should invite me to your party because I really know how to make balloons fly. We will go places in those balloons. We will! Even though it is my nature to be inert, I am NOT gravitationally bound. If you do not invite me to your party, you better watch it because WARNING! I have the lowest boiling point in the universe. So, invite me to your party today and for an added bonus, I'll make your voice go funny.

In discussing this text with students ask them where such a speech might be heard. Have they ever encountered such oratory or a monologue in literature? On television? In their community? What is the difference between this oratory and a simple testimonial? What is *Helium* asking for? Both this example and the next political speech, in which ***Stealthily*** is seeking your vote to land him in the coveted office of dogcatcher, are similar in form but differ in what they ask for (see Appendix L for projectable sample). You may wish to use both for the students to compare and contrast.

Sample Political Oratory for *Stealthily*

I, *Stealthily*, am your very best choice for dogcatcher. Vote for me on Tuesday. I have caught 99.9 percent of all animals I have set out to apprehend. Imagine that your new puppy is hiding under your porch but he is too scared to come out. I, *Stealthily*, have the ability to move without making a sound. I never crunch a twig under my feet or sneeze when I shouldn't. Unlike my clumsy opponent, *Ruckus*, who is noisy beyond compare, I am quiet as snow on the ground. I blend in with my surroundings when doing my job so I never get noticed, making me the perfect choice for the tricky position of dogcatcher. If I am elected dogcatcher all strays will be off the streets in less than a week and every new escaped dog will be caught within fifteen minutes because they will never see what got them! *Crafty*, the dogcatcher from one town over, says, "*Stealthily* is the sneakiest person I know." Vote for me if you want your loose dogs caught!

After sharing one or both of these read-alouds and guiding the class through a discussion, follow the steps in the lesson process at the end of this chapter to guide your students through completion of their persuasive speeches. In these and all the definition writings, urge students to write what they know. Keep the political speeches local (student council, mayor, treasurer of the band boosters) and advocate for local issues. This serves a variety of purposes, as students are more readily able to wrap the unfamiliar vocabulary word in references and terms with which they are already familiar and according to Beach and Doerr-Stevens, students are more motivated to write about issues where they believe they can effect some change (Beach and Doerr-Stevens 2009).

Michael: Granted, the students are writing on behalf of vocabulary words, but it always helps writers to write what they know,

Sara: Even when they are making stuff up.

In collecting some vocabulary words that we thought would work well with persuasive writing, we specifically targeted terms having to do with the genre. Please see these as starting points and add or substitute words applicable to your classroom units of study.

Tier One: Basic Words

Easier	Harder
promise	guarantee
chatter	rant
sentence	atmosphere
paragraph	verdict
audience	fortification
evidence	rival
boundary	periphery
example	soiree
detail	aspect
opinion	prohibit

Tier Two: Conceptual Words

Easier	Harder
excited	empathy
thrilled	implore
disappointed	urge
sincere	condemn
proud	vehemently
unfair	strive
manipulate	obscure
ignore	entice
belief	cite
influence	exclude
invincible	abundant
invisible	
emphasize	

Lesson Process

❶ **Share** one of the persuasive writing samples provided or another of your own choosing with your students by reading it out loud or projecting a copy.

❷ **Discuss** the qualities of persuasive writing with the class. What constitutes a strong argument? What specific language is used when trying to persuade? How are facts and opinions used to the author's advantage in order to encourage the reader or listener to agree with the sentiment presented? Which of the ten techniques listed earlier were used in the examples?

❸ **Model** the process by co-creating one of these word-pieces along with your students, with you scribing their suggestions on the board or projector. As always, we start with our Collaboration Cheat Sheet before composing our Version 1. While crafting the piece with the students it is a good idea to reinforce any patterns—for example, leading with a question—which you have discussed while introducing the genre. Leave this example and the Cheat Sheet on the board while students are working on their own pieces—this will cut down on a lot of structure questions.

❹ **Choose and collaborate.** Choose or assign vocabulary words (see Chapter 2, "Choosing the Words") for your writers or groups of writers. Persuasive writing is opinionated; expect the murmur of collaboration to be at a steady buzz as students form their arguments for or against their assigned vocabulary words. Depending on the type of persuasive writing you are using as your model, the amount of collaboration on the writing of the finished piece may vary. An editorial may lend itself to a single author while an infomercial might require several, especially during the performance portion. Either approach is fine as long as the students discuss the new word among themselves during the Cheat Sheet portion of the exercise.

❺ **Provide** vocabulary research materials for your students. Ideally this should not be limited to a classroom set of dictionaries. Take a look back at our ideas about Researching Words in the Digital Age (on page xi). It's also a very good idea to provide extra examples of persuasive writing. Remember, we spent a few minutes watching Billy Mays infomercials on YouTube before we attempted writing one. Another place to find some dramatic examples of persuasive speech would be in the summations of the closing arguments presented in courtroom dramas shows such as *Law and Order*.

❻ **Write.** Provide writing time in class. Our discussions and use of the Collaboration Cheat Sheet help students organize their facts so that the actual writing time of their piece should not be a long drawn-out affair. You may want to walk about the class and remind students that they have this support material at their disposal. You may also suggest that a good persuasive writer uses his strongest argument, and that their Cheat Sheets are a repository for a whole lot of ideas from which they may pick the strongest and leave the rest behind. If students are writing in groups or even solo, expect and encourage discussion during the writing process as students confer to clarify meanings and prioritize from their notes.

❼ **Turn and talk.** Have students share their writing out loud within their groups. Persuasive writing lends itself to be spoken out loud. Instruct the students to pay particular attention to the fluency of their pieces as they are read aloud. Does each sentence move their argument forward?

Persuasive writing often finds itself under some sort of constraint, whether a word count on an op-ed page or a time limit on a television commercial. This initial out-loud rendering is an opportunity for first edits of our Version 1.

❽ **Perform.** Have students present their persuasive pieces to the whole class. If they have been working in small groups, the whole group participates in the performance. Think late-night infomercial or a speech from the senate floor. Encourage the students to go a little bit over the top with this one. Persuasive writing and performance are passionate; remind students that they are trying to convince their audience to act in a certain way after hearing their presentation.

❾ **Assess.** Lead the class in a discussion of the writing and performance they have just experienced. Ask kids what the new vocabulary word means, what it doesn't mean. Equally important, did the students' presentation sell an idea to their audience? How likely are the listeners to follow the suggestions of the presenter?

❿ **Hazards.** One stumbling block that may occur in persuasive writing is straying from the objective. Each line should further the argument being presented and should be stated as a fact. (It is up to the discerning reader to decide whether the facts are substantially supported or not—which is another important lesson that may be prompted from this exercise.)

⓫ **Extra credit.** Persuasive writing segues into graphic advertising or a PowerPoint presentation. Students may enjoy creating print ads or a keynote speech about or by their vocabulary word. The infomercial lends itself especially well to video. This type of writing also invites written response from the listeners like letters to the editor prompted by an editorial.

High Definition Through Narrative Writing

Beginning, middle, end.
Beginning, middle, end.
Beginning, middle, end.
Say it enough, and kids will get it. Right?

Maybe. But mastering the art of storytelling (beginning, middle, and end) follows the same course that an artist takes to get to Carnegie Hall: Practice, practice, practice. Why not practice by telling the story of ***elegant***? Or cross the hall and borrow a word from social studies such as ***plague***, or ***random*** from the math class next door.

Michael: Reminds me of the story of the psychic dwarf who had escaped from prison.

Sara: Dare I ask?

Michael: He was a small medium at large!

Sara: [sigh]

What we're really talking about here is another pattern—that of narrative structure. While beginning, middle, and end is a good starting point, most stories introduce some obstacle within this blueprint—a conflict. This conflict is resolved in some fashion and the story concludes. The lead or exposition, development or rising action, conflict, resolution, and conclusion are the components of narrative structure. So how do we boil this down into an easily modeled pattern into which we may slide some vocabulary words?

Our first vocabulary word story is going to be just five sentences long. Starting with our outline, students will create an opening sentence from their initial brainstorm list (completion of the Collaboration Cheat Sheet). After this is completed they will add another declarative sentence—another good detail about the word. The third sentence in their opus will begin with the word ***unfortunately***. The following sentence begins with the word ***fortunately*** and, amazingly enough, the final sentence begins with the word ***finally***.

That's it. Basic narrative structure rendered down to five sentences. The students have written a lead with their first sentence. The second sentence provides rising action. The word *unfortunately* introduces a problem—the conflict—into their story. The word *fortunately* resolves or at least mitigates the conflict, and *finally* wraps the whole thing up (Holbrook 2005).

- First sentence . . .
- Second sentence . . .
- Unfortunately . . .
- Fortunately . . .
- Finally . . .

The best part about giving out this assignment is answering the first kid who asks, "What kind of story?" with, "Up to you. Just make it up." They look at you with wide eyes.

"Just make it up?" We tell them to go for it. Prepare yourself for zombies and space aliens with very impressive vocabularies.

Writing a Nonfiction Story

Okay, Here's What Happened

We had great success with this pattern when our teacher friends at Bay Village Middle School set us up in the sixth-grade biology classes on the day they just happened to be beginning a unit on the human reproduction system.

Michael: I think *set up* is the operative term here.

Sara: Yes. I just remember asking if we could come into the science classes to write stories about vocabulary words.

Michael: Weren't we surprised when they asked us that morning if we wanted to start with ***fallopian tubes*** or ***scrotum***?

Teachers Laurel Beck and Brent Illenberger first introduced the unit, distributing a comprehensive glossary and packet of information, including diagrams, to students. They had identified words (many Tier Three, content-specific words) that they believed required some advance work before starting the unit. We put those words on slips of paper, divided the classes into small groups, and had every group draw three words. You know the words we're talking about—***vagina***, ***testosterone***, ***estrogen***, and ***penis***—all words with a significant giggle factor, particularly in a middle school class. We began by introducing the narrative pattern with a science word from their previous unit: ***carnivore*** (see Appendix M for a projectable sample).

Carnivore: Version 1

Fact: A true *carnivore* is an animal that eats only meat.
Fact: *Carnivores* either catch their food by hunting or they scavenge meat from already dead animals.

Unfortunately, *carnivores* are killers because they have short digestive systems that are not very good at breaking down plant material.
Fortunately, *carnivores* use their claws and sharp teeth to hunt and help strengthen their prey's population by mostly eating the weak or sick.
Finally, *carnivores* kill for food and will never become vegetarians.

The students confirmed that this sample pretty much summed up some good facts about carnivores into a little nonfiction story. But, like all first drafts, we discussed how we might make the story better through revision. At that point, we revealed Version Two of our story, pared down to eliminate unnecessary words.

Carnivore: Version 2

A *carnivore* is an animal that eats only meat, catching food by hunting or scavenging.

They have short digestive systems, which don't break down plants well.

Using claws and sharp teeth, *carnivores* strengthen their prey's population by eating the weak and the sick.

We talked about how the topic sentence of the story, like any topic sentence, sets the stage for what's to follow. We talked about the word *carnivore*, examining the text for what it is and what it is not. After sharing the pattern for narrative structure with the sixth graders, we did a group write, modeling writing a story using the word ***estrogen***. Students quickly consulted their glossary materials for facts so that we could complete a Collaboration Cheat Sheet on the board. They conferred with one another and then we composed the following story taking extra care to make the last line "school appropriate."

Estrogen is a hormone.
It is found in the female body.
Fortunately, it is found in the male body, too.
Unfortunately, it often causes unpredictable changes.
Finally, it gives women their shapes.

Michael: Hey, we mixed up the unfortunately/fortunately part of the story.

Sara: Ideas were coming fast. I was just trying to keep up with the writing.

Michael: Actually, it doesn't matter as long as the conflict is in the narrative.

After we wrote a Version 1, we revised to make Version 2 with fewer words. This step serves two purposes: It helps students prioritize which are the most important elements of the story and it forces them to write the story twice, thereby reinforcing the meaning of the word.

Working in a small group after research and with much discussion, Ginny, Daniella, Jen, and Katie wrote three fortunately/unfortunately stories defining ***puberty***, ***scrotum***, and ***sterile***.

Brent and Laurel both observed that introducing this unit through our writing and performance vocabulary activities took a lot of the sting out of the words in addition to giving the students the background knowledge necessary to understand the unit. We observed how the teachers had carefully planned for this unit, providing glossaries and support materials (with illustrations). These tools supplied much more thorough information than simple dictionary definitions. The students' finished pieces of writing also served as a means for the teachers to assess prior knowledge of these terms. The word *sterile* is not really adequately defined in the student's writing (see Figure 5.2), for instance. It is defined in terms of *what* happens when a person (male or female) is sterile, but it does not explain *why* or *how* it happens. This information was vital to Brent and Laurel in their course development.

Figure 5.1 **Estrogen** *Narrative with Revisions*

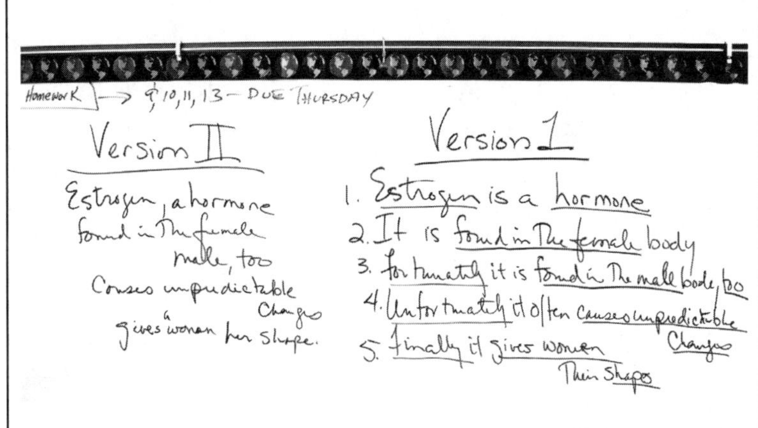

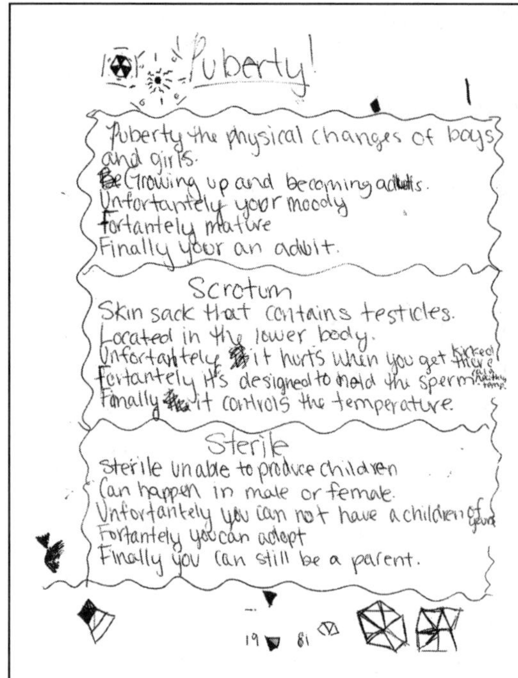

Puberty!

Puberty the physical changes of boys and girls.
Growing up and becoming adults.
Unfortantely your moody
Fortantely mature
Finally your an adult.

Scrotum

Skin sack that contains testicles.
Located in the lower body.
Unfortantely it hurts when you get kicked there
Fortantely it's designed to hold the sperm
Finally it controls the temperature.

Sterile

Sterile unable to produce children
Can happen in male or female.
Unfortantely you can not have a children of your
Fortantely you can adopt
Finally you can still be a parent.

1981

Figure 5.2 *Ginny, Daniella, Jen, and Katie's Fortunately/Unfortunately Stories*

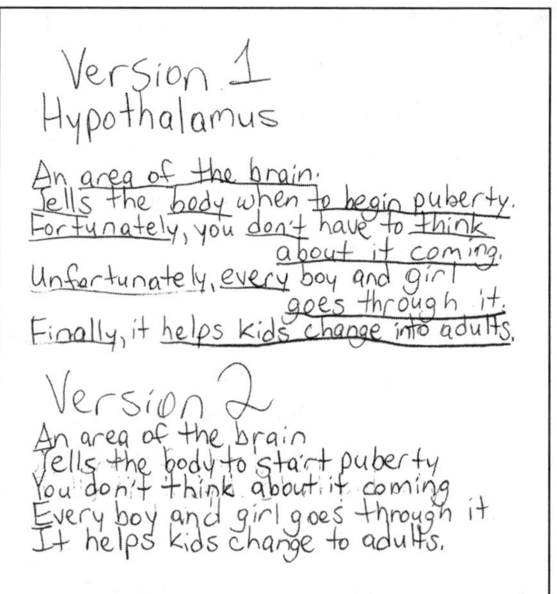

Version 1
Hypothalamus

An area of the brain.
Tells the body when to begin puberty.
Fortunately, you don't have to think about it coming.
Unfortunately, every boy and girl goes through it.
Finally, it helps kids change into adults.

Version 2

An area of the brain
Tells the body to start puberty
You don't think about it coming
Every boy and girl goes through it
It helps kids change to adults.

Figure 5.3 *Gail's Narrative for* **Hypothalamus**

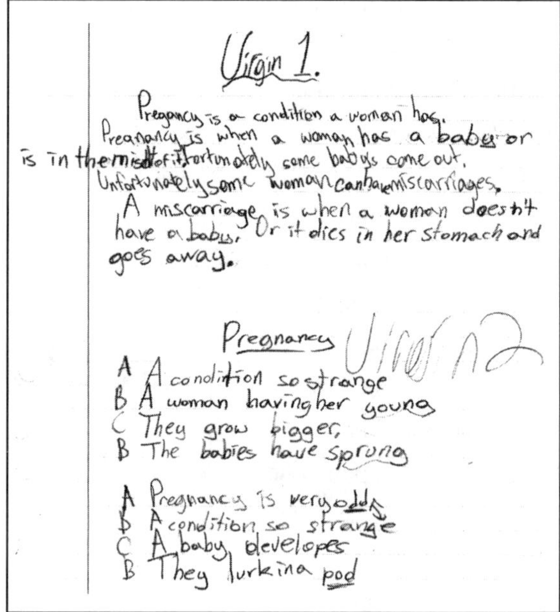

Virgin 1.

Pregancy is a condition a woman has.
Preganancy is when a woman has a baby or is in the midst of it. Fortunately some babys come out.
Unfortunately some woman can have miscarriages.
A miscarriage is when a woman doesn't have a baby. Or it dies in her stomach and goes away.

Pregnancy
Virgin 2

A A condition so strange
B A woman having her young
C They grow bigger,
B The babies have sprung

A Pregnancy is very odd
B A condition so strange
C A baby developes
B They lurk in a pod

Figure 5.4 *Revised Story*

Sara: We found the sample in Figure 5.4 after we had left the classroom. Note the rendering of Version 1 and Version 2.

Michael: Hopefully, this written definition of ***pregnancy*** was resolved by the end of the unit.

Sara: I have confidence in Laurel and Brent.

Writing Fiction

Here's What Could Have Happened

In science class we were working on nonfiction narratives, but fiction is functional, too. Our science word stories turned out to be very factual, thanks in part to the nature of the words and because of the wealth of research material provided to the students by the teachers. But what about terms pulled from a novel? We continued our vocabulary story crafting in the sixth-grade language arts classroom across the hall. The students, who were all part of the same block, were already familiar with basic narrative structure through the use of the unfortunately/fortunately pattern introduced to them in science class. Who says science and art don't mix?

We took this opportunity to up the ante a little bit. First, we shared our example for the word ***elation*** (see Appendix N for a projectable sample).

Elation: Version 1

Sentence 1: *Elation* was so happy it won the tournament that it screamed like a siren and jumped up straight in the air.
Sentence 2: Totally excited, it laughed and clapped and could not calm down.
Unfortunately, it couldn't act somber or get serious and got in trouble for making so much noise.
Fortunately, the outburst didn't last long and luckily *Elation* avoided getting a penalty for showboating.
Finally, *Elation* skipped outside where it could really enjoy itself.

After we shared our sample, we filled out a Collaboration Cheat Sheet for one of the challenging words, ***resistance***, from Christopher Paul Curtis' *The Watsons Go to Birmingham—1963*. With the students researching the word meaning and offering ideas, together we wrote a fictional narrative for *resistance*.

> *Resistance* liked to fight back against her parents.
> She refused to do the dishes when it was her turn.
> *Unfortunately*, the dishes would get all crusty, making more work.
> *Fortunately*, she didn't break the dishes because she was nonviolent.
> *Finally*, she had to work twice as hard to get the dishes clean.

Notice we did not try to re-create a scene out of the novel for our story definition of *resistance*. Instead we took the word *resistance* out of the novel and brought it home to familiar territory to see how it would act, creating an authentic but fictional narrative in which *resistance* refuses to do her chores.

We noticed that the challenge words from the novel were slightly different than the ones we had encountered across the hall at our laminated lab tables in the science classroom. The vocabulary words here tended for the most part to be Tier Two concept words, with far fewer as content specific as, say, *hypothalamus*. We found that these language arts words lent themselves a bit more easily to personification, turning our subject matter into characters who managed to get themselves into all kinds of trouble.

Figure 5.5 *Fictional Narrative for* **Resistance**

FIGHTS BACK HOLDS ITS ground REFUSE TO FOLLOW RULES BE SNEAKY & SILENT THROW THINGS STUBBORN NON VIOLENT CAN BE RIGHT	RESISTANCE LIKES TO FIGHT BACK AGAINST HER ~~ITS~~ PARENTS SHE REFUSED TO DO THE DISHES WHEN IT WAS HER TURN UNFORTUNATELY THE DISHES WOULD GET ALL CRUSTY, MAKING MORE WORK
DOORMAT DOESN'T GIVE UP NOT ALWAYS RIGHT DOESN'T WORRY ABOUT PEOPLE PLEASING	FORTUNATELY SHE DIDN'T BREAK THE DISHES BECAUSE SHE WAS NON-VIOLENT FINALLY SHE HAD TO WORK TWICE AS HARD TO GET THE DISHES CLEAN.

Since our students already knew the basic story structure premise—rising action, conflict, resolution, and conclusion—we challenged them to complete the assignment sans the words *unfortunately* and *fortunately*. We shared our Version Two of our *elation* piece, where the pattern words had been stripped as part of the paring-down process. We instructed the students to think of the concepts *unfortunately* and *fortunately* as they composed their very short pieces of vocabulary word fiction (see Appendix N for a projectable sample).

Elation: Version 2

Elation won the tournament! It screamed like a siren and jumped in the air, totally excited.

Elation couldn't calm down, act serious or somber.

No penalty for showboating, *Elation* skipped away.

Figure 5.6 *Kendall's* **Equally** *Piece*

Equally

Equally was walking down a very buisy street wearing just a sweat shirt and jeans. It was Saturday morning and new York City was very crowded. Equally saw a couple of Kids fighting over a piece of gum. He dashed over to the Kids a kneeled down beside them. He explain to them how to be equal. There were 6 pieces of gum and 3 Kids. Equally started out giving each Kid 1 piece of gum. after he had done that there were only 3 pieces left. when he passed out all of the pieces of gum every Kid had two pieces of gum. That tells you about his soft side.

Kendall's piece about ***equally*** has no mention of the pattern words we started out with, but the conflict is certainly easy to find. Three kids arguing over a pack of gum. *Equally*, being the impartial mediator that he is, solves this dilemma by portioning out the treats, well, *equally*. Does Kendall understand the term *equally* and its subcontext as a means of conflict resolution? She certainly does, and she also understands narrative structure. Once students have mastered this stripped-down narrative story structure, they can go on to write more complex stories, diary entries, and personal narratives.

Writing Journal and Diary Entries

Note to Self

What keeps ***Apprehensive*** up at night? And why is ***Oblivious*** sleeping like a baby? Not like a real baby that screams at two in the morning, but one of those little cherubs in commercials that slumbers in peace as the parent flips off the light switch. What happened in the course of the day and how did that the word respond? If a word kept a diary, what would be a typical entry?

Diary entries are personal reflections, reactions, and promises for change. The author gives the reader a first-person account in his or her own voice. Diary entries are first-person narratives, notes to self. As such, perhaps more than any other writing genre, they are a good place for student writers to sharper their use of voice. In order to write a journal entry for a vocabulary word, a writer needs to determine if this word speaks using poor grammar, lofty phrasing, sarcasm, or baby talk. Is it apologetic or aggressive? Who is this word and what would it write about in the privacy of a journal? What are the word's dreams placed undercover?

One thing is for certain: A journal or diary entry requires plenty of detail in the writing to ensure that the writer's response is logical to the reader. *Apprehensive* may have lost a night's sleep chewing her nails, but unless the writer explains why she's all in a fret, it's not a good entry.

In Katie Lufkin's sixth-grade language arts unit on the novel *The Outsiders* by S. E. Hinton (1967), students took on writing diary entries for some of the issue-related words referenced in the book. First, Katie identified the words with input from her students. These were words the students were interested in learning more about as well as the ones that Katie knew they needed to know to understand the context of the story. The kids understood how the words were used in the novel as the characters struggled amidst and against the recurring violence between the Socials (Socs) and the Greasers.

> ***Sara:*** "Greaser" is a term that got hung on kids when I was in high school. That was—*ahem*—a few years ago.
>
> ***Michael:*** Even though the terminology is out of date, twenty-first-century kids at Bay Village Middle School had no trouble recognizing it as a stereotype. That concept, unfortunately, lives on.

The Outsiders is a powerful story. The lessons embedded in the narrative truly come to life when the readers take the terminology of S. E. Hinton, words like ***prejudice*** and ***stereotyping***, and apply them to their own lives. Here is the sample diary entry that we wrote and shared with the students to begin the lesson (see Appendix O for a projectable sample).

Private Parts

You read MY journal?
Off MY shelf?
MY dreams placed undercover?
Conversations with MYself?

That's where I go to yell
and no one's yelling back.
Where I reach my hand out
and know it won't get smacked.

That's where I go for confidence.
Where I can practice and rehearse.
My spot out of the spotlight.
Where no one tells me not to curse.

I thought I was playing safely
You peeped!
It's where my thoughts reside.
You thief!
You should have knocked
and let me dress
and come outside.

Sara Holbrook (1996)

Sample Diary Entry for *Nonconformist*

Today began with another bowl of Cheerios, just like yesterday and the day before. I boarded the bus at 7:30 A.M., right on schedule. All the rest of the kids on the bus were dressed identically—hooded sweatshirts and blue jeans, ragged at the edges and hanging down over their sneakers. Everything was the same.

Why does life have to be so monotonous? For instance, why can't some school buses in the United States be red or purple? Everywhere you go in this country the buses are yellow. Boring!

I crave something different. Life should be like a bouquet of wildflowers or at least a pile of multicolored gravel. Tomorrow I am not wearing the usual school uniform of jeans and a sweatshirt. I pledge to distinguish myself from everyone else. Tomorrow I will wear a prom dress to school or maybe a tuxedo. I will tie feathers to my ears and paint my face with glitter. Tomorrow I will just say *no* to conformity.

Signed,
Nonconformist

We discussed how the diary entry should take place during a typical single day (no life stories) and should reflect a true experience that logically may have happened during that day. Then we divided up the words among Katie's students for them to write diary entries on behalf of some of words such as ***minority***, ***majority***, ***stereotype***, ***diversity***, ***labels***, ***liberty***, ***prejudice***, and ***tolerance***. Because diary entries are naturally written by individuals, the students conferred in small table groups about the word meanings while they completed the Collaboration Cheat Sheets and then wrote their diary entries as individuals, which worked well in this class. You may choose to keep the students in groups. You know your students best.

In order to really speak for these words, we began by envisioning each word as if it were a real person. The students discussed with one another how certain words might look, what they would wear, how they would act. While these discussions were taking place, Katie and both of us circulated about the room, prompting students with questions such as:

Ⓠ What might bother *Minority*?
Ⓐ Feeling left out.

Ⓠ What would *Majority* wear?
Ⓐ Jeans and a hoodie just like everyone else.

Ⓠ What would *Tolerance* be like as a friend?
Ⓐ Forgiving.

This gave students an opportunity to come to agreement on what kind of real-life situation in which this word might be involved. In the sample word diary entry for *stereotype*, you see in the writer's prewrite that he first envisioned the word to be a skater, dressed in black, and then went on to describe a "day in the life" and an incident with a cop (Figure 5.7).

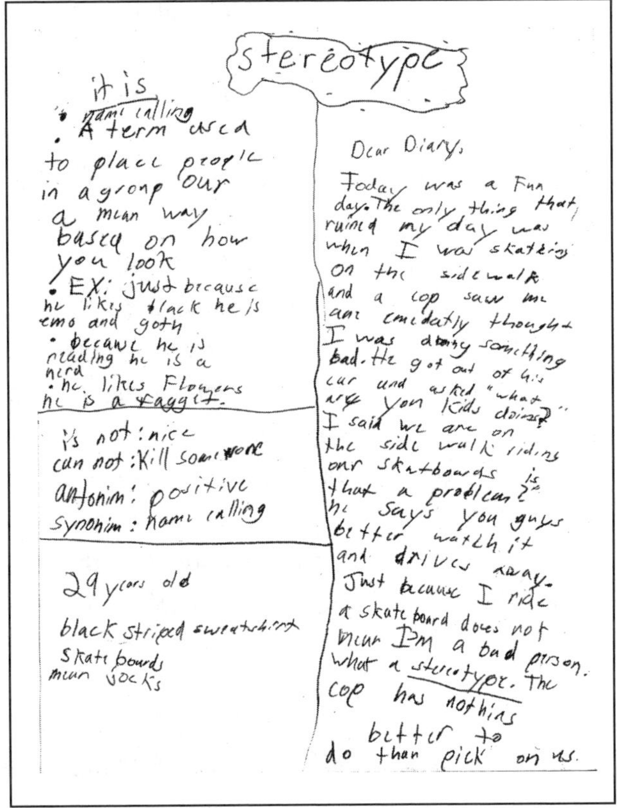
stereotype

it is
• name calling
• A term used to place people in a group our a mean way based on how you look
• EX: just because he likes black he is emo and goth
• because he is reading he is a nerd
• he likes Flowers he is a faggit.

its not: nice
can not: Kill someone
antonim: positive
synonim: name calling

29 years old
black striped sweatshirt
skate boards
mean looks

Dear Diary,
Today was a Fun day. The only thing that ruined my day was when I was skating on the sidewalk and a cop saw me and emidatly thought I was doing something bad. He got out of his car and asked "what are you kids doing?" I said we are on the side walk riding our skatbowrds is that a problem?" he says you guys better watch it and drives away. Just because I ride a skate board does not mean I'm a bad person. What a stereotype. The cop has nothing better to do than pick on us.

Figure 5.7 *Sixth-Grade Diary Entry with Prewrite*

This was one of the most popular of all the definition writing that we did with students. They loved making up stories about the words. These stories can even be edited to create a poem (Holbrook and Salinger 2006).

After the students had written their diary entries, they took turns performing them aloud. We began the performance segment as we often do, with everyone standing and reading in unison.

Sara: Well, not exactly unison. They are each reading different texts at the same time.

Michael: We have them read it once and then over again in a louder voice. It gets the students used to the sound of their own voices as well as smoothing out their reading of the text.

Sara: We have them hold the paper or notebook in one hand and then use the free hand to help tell the story.

Michael: As soon as they free up that extra hand, we hear more expression come into the reading.

After breaking the ice with the cacophony of voices, we had the students read as individuals. As the students performed, one of us interjected this question after each reading: *Now, what does that word mean? What is it not?* Since we had limited the number of words selected for diary entries, we had multiple students working on each word, which provided for some good comparisons. These discussions are quick and simply serve to reinforce the meaning of the word to the rest of the classroom audience.

As students compose their vocabulary narratives, remind them to include synonyms and at least one antonym. Satisfying a combined goal of strengthening the students' understanding of the words and concepts and their skills in narrative, the lesson is made more meaningful and memorable for everyone. What follows are some vocabulary words that might work well with these narrative-writing activities, along with some guidelines for how to make this work in your class.

●●● Tier One: Basic Words

Easier	*Harder*
plot	contrive
character	intrigue
introduction	discount
conclusion	gadget
problem	finale
adventure	prologue
setting	essence
journal	appliance
blast	conflict
escalate	authority

Tier Two: Concept Words

Easier	*Harder*
vague	unspecified
dramatic	vivid
sway	peculiar
thrill	craven
weary	pertinent
frequent	expanse
converse	massive
remain	squalor
puzzled	hectic
gawk	hoax

Lesson Process

❶ **Share** samples of narratives with your students by reading them out loud and/or projecting the text. You may use our samples from the appendices or you may decide to choose other models.

❷ **Discuss** the qualities of the genre with the class. Identify the beginning, middle, and end (introduction, conflict, resolution) of the piece while sharing with the students. What role does conflict play in narrative? Can you switch the order around and still have a story that makes sense? Reiterate that a good narrative is a self-contained piece of writing.

❸ **Model** the process by co-creating a narrative along with your students, with you scribing their suggestions on the board or projector. We start with our Collaboration Cheat Sheet to organize our brainstorm. We have found that the fortunately/unfortunately exercise works well as an initial introduction to the narrative genre. Leave your finished work on the board while students are working on their own as an example for their reference.

❹ **Choose and collaborate.** Choose or assign vocabulary words (see Chapter 2, "Choosing the Words") for your writers or groups of writers. Narratives naturally tend to lean toward the longer side. But they also encourage collaboration as students add to their stories as they talk back and forth during the crafting portion of their writing process.

❺ **Provide** vocabulary research materials for your students. This should not be limited to a classroom set of dictionaries; any good researcher always checks with multiple sources. Take a look back at our ideas about Researching Words in the Digital Age (on page xi). You may find it useful to provide collections of short narratives to augment the sample created during the modeling portion of this lesson. There are many collections available under the subgenre headings of flash fiction, sudden fiction, micro-fiction, and short-short stories, in which students can find examples for themselves.

❻ **Write.** Provide writing time in class. Once the narrative structure is understood, the writing portion will not take too long. Fifteen minutes or so should be enough time to finish Version 1 of a piece. We've frontloaded the lesson with prewriting during the Collaboration Cheat Sheet and through the introduction of the fortunately/unfortunately mode of thinking while composing the story. This is a genre that particularly benefits from a prewriting outline and oral discussion before composition.

❼ **Turn and talk.** Students may wish to just hand their papers to a neighbor for them to read. This is no good—we want them to read their work out loud to another human being. If the students have been collaborating, we have found it is useful to instruct them to read their story to someone who has not already heard or had a hand in crafting it. This gives the piece new ears, which will be more likely to notice any gaps in the narrative. Asking, "Who likes the story they have written?" will usually return a smattering of raised hands. The follow-up question, "Who likes the story they just heard?" will elicit an almost universally positive response and grease the wheels for the next step of the lesson.

❽ **Perform.** Invite students to present their word-pieces to the whole class. Storytelling is an age-old human activity. You may want to preface their performances with a discussion of the art's place in the development of human culture. Or better yet, set students to that task and invite them to join this venerable tradition. Ask them who is the best storyteller that they personally know—is it a grandfather, a neighbor, maybe one of their friends? What makes this person a good storyteller? Can the student incorporate some of the trade secrets employed by the expert storyteller that they know?

9 **Assess.** Lead the class in a discussion of the writing and performance they have just experienced. Ask kids what they think the new vocabulary word means, what it doesn't mean. Can the students identify the conflict in the story, the resolution?

10 **Hazards.** We want to avoid the bed-to-bed kind of stories that read like a list. I got up, then I brushed my teeth, then I put on my clothes, then I ate breakfast . . . Remember *unfortunately*—what is the conflict in the story? What provides the resolution? Another thing to watch for is that students may really get into their stories and sometimes forget to include an antonym for their vocabulary word.

11 **Extra credit.** We like to use the performance section of this exercise to show kids how the sequence of stories can be changed. Repeatedly we have heard from teachers (and editors, we might add) that some students don't understand stories if they are not in chronological order. This is a particular challenge for struggling readers. Since all stories (insert movies, television shows, and plays) do not come in perfect sequence, it's beneficial to show kids how they can reconstruct their own stories. We like to do this in performance using a trick we learned and adapted from veteran educator/author/fun person Nancy Steineke (2009). Have five students stand before the class and read a fortunately/unfortunately story, each student reciting one line. Have the rest of the class practice

rearranging the readers (and thereby the story) and see how understandable the story is no matter what the order of the sentences.

> ***Michael:*** When using the fortunately/unfortunately pattern to teach narrative, I like to have the students skip a line between sentences. That way we can mix up the order afterward.
>
> ***Sara:*** It may take a little tweaking.
>
> ***Michael:*** But usually we are able to create a story that still makes sense.
>
> ***Sara:*** Like the French filmmaker Jean-Luc Godard said, "A story should have a beginning, middle, and end—but not necessarily in that order."

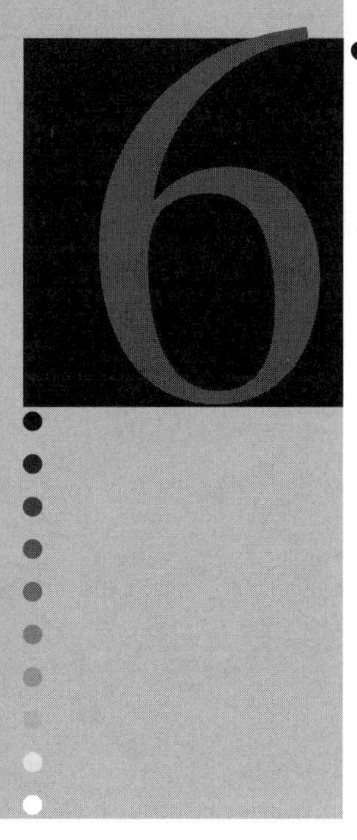

High Definition Through Descriptive Writing

Sara: The sunset was pretty.

Michael: Can you be more specific?

Sara: The sunset was gorgeous.

Michael: More specific.

Sara: The sunset was super-fantastic-outta-this-world fabulous.

Ever have a conversation like this with a student? This is typical of dialogues we have in classrooms in response to student writers' efforts at description. Piling on subjective terms or, as we explain them to students, opinion words, does little to bring an image to the reader's mind. "My brother is weird. This ice cream is good. That car is cool," they write and then ask, "See what I mean?" And the answer is, of course, "no." Absent any sensory language, how can we? Vibrant descriptions are what make historical figures and events come to life in our fiction and nonfiction alike. Descriptions help us visualize a twenty-foot anaconda, hear the thunder of stampeding buffalo on the open plain, and smell the campfires of Lewis and Clark. Descriptive language makes us want to dig deeper and learn more. Learning to craft sensory descriptions will help us in our content-area reading and writing.

Maybe descriptive writing is not specifically delineated as part of the English language arts standards in your state. Maybe (gasp) it's not on "the test." Does that mean we can afford to skip coaching students in how to shape clear, evocative descriptions?

Crafting sense-evoking language is applicable across all writing genres; it is a skill that needs to be honed on its own and utilized as needed. Learning to write a detailed and descriptive text is learning how to illustrate with words. This is how we show evidence to back up our opinions. How we prove our points. You might say the ability to capture an image and put it into words is at the heart of all writing. A writing coach can say, "Show, don't tell" from now until the sun sets, but until students learn to describe "how" something looks, sounds, tastes, smells, and feels they are never going to be able to compose a gripping story, give accurate accident testimony, or explicitly report on cell division. Of course, adding a little vocabulary acquisition along with this opportunity for creativity and deeper thinking gives descriptive writing exercises a practicality that quells even the most test-centric administrator's reservations.

Nobel Prize–winner Octavio Paz distinguishes between a descriptive passage and a narrative by drawing an analogy to visual art: "No painting can tell a story because nothing happens in it . . . in paintings things simply *are*; they do not *happen*. To speak and to write, to tell stories and to think is to experience time elapsing, to go from one place to another: to advance" (Paz 1990). Like a painting, descriptive writing can just *be*. Here we are not worried about beginning, middle, and end; we are practicing the art of enhancing our writing with colorful, aromatic, and tactile details.

Because kids love to tell stories, we found it useful to spend some time discussing the difference between a descriptive passage and a full story. A descriptive passage explains the color and design of the dress before we try and persuade someone to buy it. It tells the reader how the sun reflects off the water right before we dive into the pool in our narrative. This is an important distinction that can be made with students to improve their writing in other content areas. In science, this is the difference between evidence and interpretation (Holbrook 2005), what something is versus what we surmise about it. In social studies, it is the difference between a yellow-red glow of a city on fire and the moral interpretations of *Gone with the Wind*. We describe exactly what we see (the evidence) leaving our opinions, the whys and what-ifs, for later analysis. Descriptive passages are objective. As writers, we do our best to re-create a scene or an instant in time so that our reader is empowered to find personal meaning seemingly with no direction from us as writers but through their own experience and prior knowledge. If opinion words (***weird***, ***lovely***, ***horrible***) are used, they must be so immersed in supporting descriptive details as to make them irrefutable.

Ray Bradbury advises writers to "Put two and two on the page but not add it up for their reader" (Bradbury 1990). This is our goal. Rather than describing ***reluctant*** with another single word like ***wary***, we want our students to tell us about *Reluctant*'s having its fingers pried one by one from the door jamb as it is dragged into the room. The optimal question descriptive writers need to ask themselves is: Can I picture this in my head, what sounds am I hearing, what smells, and what does it feel like? This lesson is a good opportunity to instill the notion that imagery includes all the senses, not just what we can see.

If the end goal of descriptive writing is to depict a person, place, or thing by utilizing strong sensory language, then the means are details, details, details. What follows are some samples of how to work with students to develop a description of a person, place, and thing—descriptive components that students may then use to enhance their persuasive, explanatory, and narrative prose.

Writing Character Descriptions

Who Goes There?

Katie Lufkin and her teaching partner, Sherri Deal, had both observed that their sixth-grade students needed a boost in learning how to write character descriptions. "Every time I ask sixth graders for a character description," Katie reported, "the kids give me a plot summary." Learning to read and write detailed character descriptions not only helps kids in their reading comprehension in fictional literature, it also will help nonfiction come to life as we begin to picture historical figures and events.

Your library has plenty of nonfiction picture book character descriptions, no doubt. A couple of our favorites are two by Pam Muñoz Ryan, *When Marian Sang: The True Recital of Marian Anderson* and *Amelia and Eleanor Go for a Ride*. But these are only two examples from shelves of biographical picture books in your library. If you are looking for character description models, choose a picture book in your library and read it aloud. Have the students identify descriptive language that tells us the age, gender, talents, and culture of the character. Not the story of Amelia Earhart's flight, but the characteristics she had that enabled her to fly against the norms of her time.

Figure 6.1 *Writing in a Sixth-Grade Math Class*

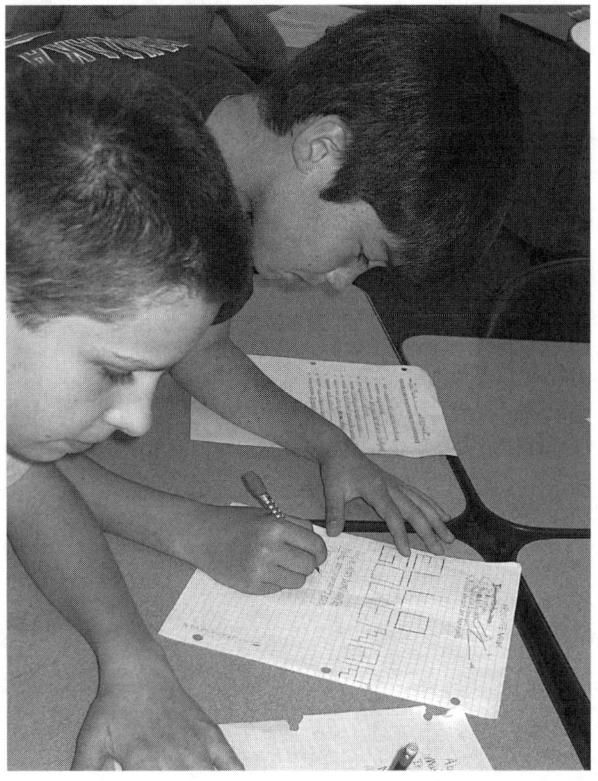

Bay Middle School operates on a block scheduling plan, so after Katie and Sherri briefed us on the sixth graders' need to learn how to write a character description, we decided to help their students—not in language arts, but in Mark Kevesdy's math classes (same kids, same block, different content area). In some of Mark's classes we had written narratives (see Chapter 5), but this time we made it clear we were just going to describe a math word as a person. Mark has his students write throughout the year, so putting sentences together in math class didn't seem at all strange to the kids.

Here again, we are asking our students to surround their new words with phrases and descriptions of their own construction. Mark had pulled together a list of vocabulary words he considered vital for students to know before leaving the sixth grade.

ratio	random	inverse operation
proportion	absolute value	certain
similar polygons	possible	chance
rate	probable	sequence
variable	expression	event
integers	equation	

It was May and our vocabulary writing served as a way for students to discuss in small groups some of the terms they had used throughout the year, reteaching and reminding one another of the meanings. Their written artifacts became a way for Mark to assess their understanding.

Sara: What immediately struck me about this list is how these words were not only important to understanding math, but understanding life. It was fun to talk about how *Random* and *Certain* would dress differently, what their professions might be, and their goals for the future.

Michael: In the language of Beck, McKeown, and Kucan (2002), these are Tier Two concept words—useful not only in math but in other content areas as well.

Sara: It was precisely those double-duty words we were talking about in Chapter 2, "Choosing the Words."

Along with Mark, we chose about six of the words for students to use in writing character descriptions. First, we projected a character description for the word ***flamboyant***. (See Appendix P for a projectable sample.)

Character Descripton for *Flamboyant*

Flamboyant is a pink flamingo flapping in the lunchroom. She wears feathers in her hair and giant gold earrings. She is not shy and prefers singing to whispering. She wears rhinestones on her high-tops and purple eye shadow, and paints her nails lime green. *Flamboyant* is never mousy or plain. Instead she prefers to twirl through life, tap dancing to the tune "If My Friends Could See Me Now."

Sara: We began the discussion by asking the students if any teacher had ever asked them to "show, don't tell."

Michael: I could hear their eyes rolling.

Sara: Sixth graders specialize in eye rolls. The show-don't-tell thing is a bit more of a challenge.

We began by asking some leading questions, like: Did we say *Flamboyant* was weird? Did we judge her or describe her? What's the difference? What about her appearance communicates what kind of person *Flamboyant* is? What words tell us who she is not? And then to open students up to additional possibilities for descriptors: could *Flamboyant* be a boy? We wanted the students to tell us how their vocabulary word would move, act, and react. We let the students know they would get to play dress up with the new words and make them strut around a bit and that descriptions can come in the form of a paragraph, a poem, or even a detailed sentence.

After that, the students broke into groups of two and three and the words were dealt out like playing cards by Mark (aka Mr. K.). In passing out the words he noted that it was ***probable*** that all groups would receive a word to define, but that the distribution was ***random*** and the word they received was simply a matter of ***chance***, humorously putting the words into play. The students got busy completing their Collaboration Cheat Sheets (Appendix A).

What followed were not narratives, but rather detail-oriented depictions of the characters that allow readers to infer the nature of the word being described—*Random* incongruously wearing rain boots on a sunny day, *Chance* peering from under a poker visor, and ***Event*** making sure that everyone knows about its presence—all evoke sensory images that carry memorable meaning. By having more than one writer, or more than one group of writers, defining the same word through their character descriptions, we were able to compare and contrast the definitions in the discussions after the classroom performance, further imprinting the meaning on the rest of the class.

Figure 6.2 *Megan's* **Random** *Poem*

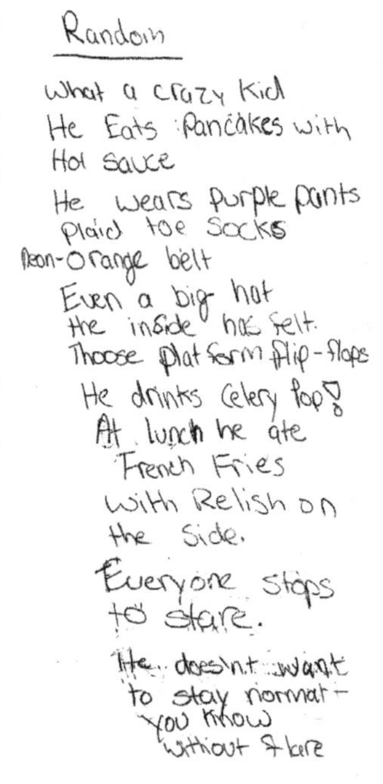

All students made two versions of their descriptions. Zach was able to get even more detail into his Version 2, while Megan used the opportunity to turn her description into a poem (see Figure 6.2).

In Sarah's writing, she used her first draft (Version 1) to describe the character *Event* with specific details, giving her the profession of an actress who's "always causing things to happen." Notice in her second draft (Version 2) she inserts that character into a little narrative where, indeed, *Event* makes things happen (see Figure 6.4 on page 114). During the performance part of the lesson, some of the students were quick to notice that Sarah had put her character in a story.

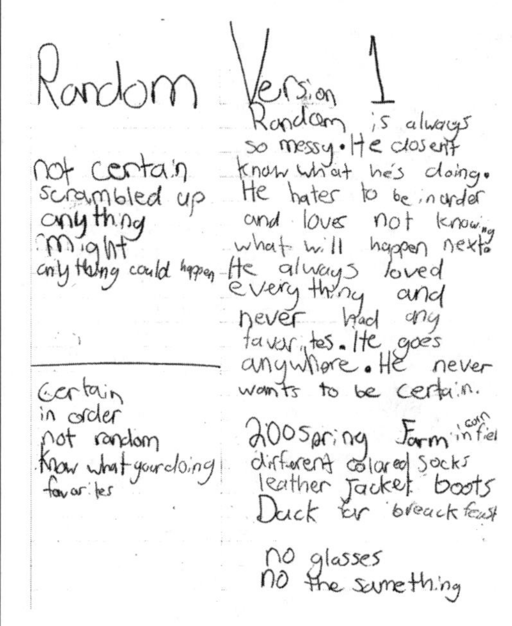
Random Version 1

not certain
scrambled up
anything
might
any thing could happen

Random is always so messy. He dosen't know what he's doing. He hates to be in order and loves not knowing what will happen next. He always loved every thing and never had any favorites. He goes anywhere. He never wants to be certain.

certain
in order
not random
know what your doing
favorites

2:00 spring Farm corn in fiel
different colored socks
leather Jacket boots
Duck for breackfeast

no glasses
no the samething

Figure 6.3a *Zach's Version 1 Character Description*

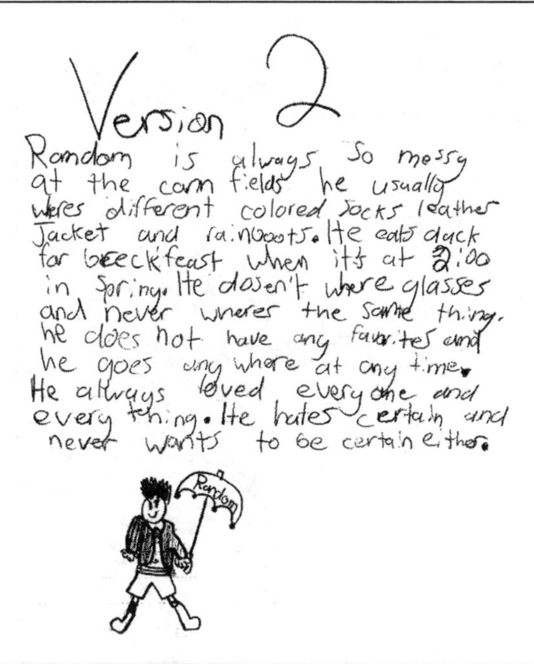
Version 2

Random is always so messy at the corn fields he usually weres different colored socks leather Jacket and rainboots. He eats duck for breeckfeast when it's at 2:00 in spring. He dosen't where glasses and never wheres the same thing. he does not have any favorites and he goes any where at any time. He always loved every one and every thing. He hates certain and never wants to be certain either.

Figure 6.3b *Zach's Version 2 Character Description*

Michael: We did not say what she had done was wrong; we just used that as an opportunity to reteach the difference between a description and a narrative.

Sara: That's right. The important thing is that students come away from the lesson with (1) a better understanding of the vocabulary word, and (2) a better understanding of descriptive writing.

We took the same exercise into Libby Royko's eighth-grade classroom where they were collectively reading *To Kill a Mockingbird*. We had put the words on slips of paper and students drew their words out of basket. Kelsey and Rachel chose the word ***corpulent*** to outfit and examine. The girls used both the dictionary and the thesaurus to

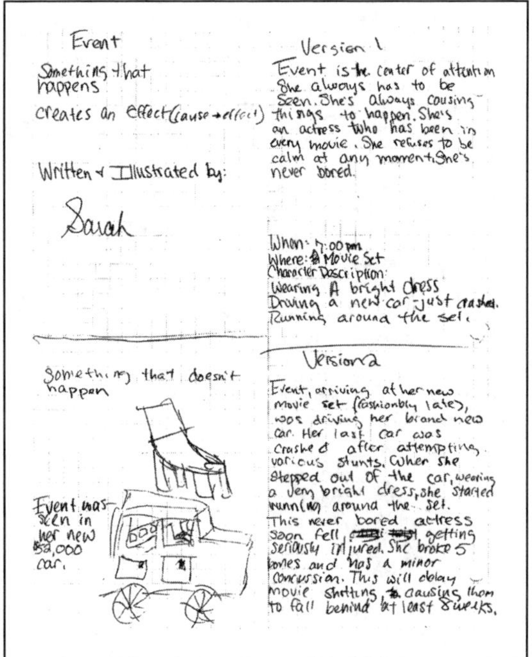

Figure 6.4 *Sarah's* **Character** *Description*

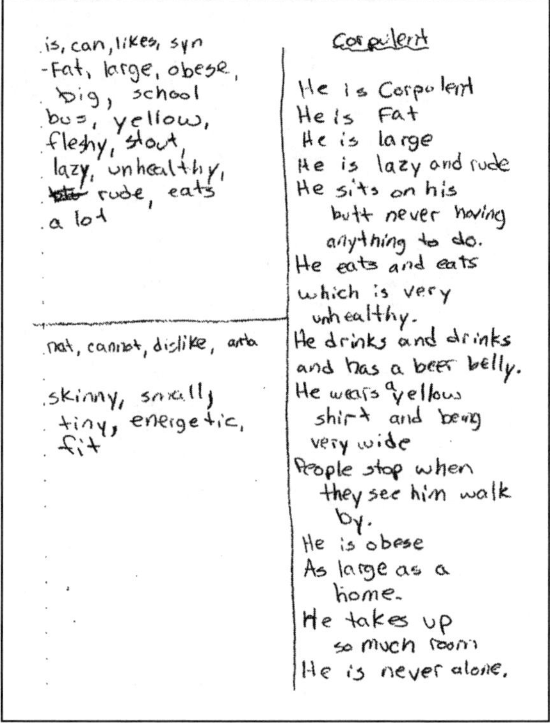

Figure 6.5 *Kelsey and Rachel's Collaboration Cheat Sheet for* **Corpulent**

research what *corpulent* is and what it is not in order to complete their Collaboration Cheat Sheet (Appendix A). You can see how collecting the synonyms during the prewrite contributed to *Corpulent*'s beer belly (see Figure 6.5). In the performance part of the lesson Libby asked if it was true that *Corpulent* is never alone, whereupon the writers explained that they were saying that *Corpulent* is so fat that he is never alone, something that the kids in the room all seemed to believe made total sense but left us adults wondering. But even a little disagreement can be a good thing since all discussion about these vocabulary words is effective as it serves to reinforce the whole class' understanding of the word meaning.

Writing Place or Object Descriptions

My Bedroom Looked Like a Blast Zone

In the case of a sunrise or a sunset, colorful details come in pretty handy. Consider Emily Dickinson's description of a sunset. "... How He [the sun] set, I know not. There seemed a purple stile, / which little yellow boys and girls were climbing all the while. / Till when they reached the other side, / A dominie in gray / Put gently up the evening bars, / — And led the flock away" (Dickinson 1951, poem 151). No subjective or opinion words at all (it was lovely, colorful, patient), but rather a vivid image personifying the earth's rotation as a schoolmaster leading his pupils away for the evening.

Literature runs rampant with sunset descriptions. In fact, though, descriptive paragraphs need *not* be linked to landscapes, sunsets, or images of picturesque lighthouses and mountain ranges—places that may be foreign and unfamiliar to our students. Just as we all have a limited tolerance for other people's vacation pictures, kids are reluctant to engage in descriptive writing about places they've never seen.

It can be just as effective (probably more so) for students to work from what they know—pictures of the insides of their lockers or the glove compartment of the family car—and formulate a precise description. Combining the genre of descriptive writing with vocabulary instruction is a natural pairing since it is specific word choice that really clarifies an image. (See Appendix Q for a projectable sample.)

Sample Descripton of a Place for *Extravagant*

A visit to *Extravagant*'s crib reveals that he owns the most modern, most expensive condo on the Gold Coast. Behind the solid mahogany door is an entryway, which is floored in black marble. Overhead is a twirling mirrored ball reflecting 10,000 lights mounted in the ceiling and surrounding walls. His living room, kitchen, and bedroom glow in shades of gold proving that he does not know the meaning of the word *economical*. His bathroom is bigger than the average living room. The sunken bath is topped with gold-plated fixtures sparkling in the sun pouring through the skylight. Standing like a throne against the back wall is a toilet with a heated seat with digital controls on the arm rests. Some might say that his crib is pretty gaudy, but one thing is for sure, *Extravagant* laid out some major cash to outfit his crib. He is definitely not cheap or stingy. *Extravagant*'s crib is just like he is, over the top.

This scene could just as easily have been set in *Extravagant*'s ride (a Hummer stretch limo?) or seated at his dinner table, which would of course be overflowing with mounds of shrimp and lobster. In your discussion of this sample, you might ask about other places a word might go. Where would it vacation—***Reticent*** in the basement, ***Intrepid*** on Everest? Kelsey and Rachel described *Corpulent* as a person, but what would his dinner table look like? Describe the landscape of ***Emaciated***. Write a model together as a group and kids will have the concept down in no time.

Some things are married to almost coloring-book images: ***parrot***, ***pyramid***, ***piranha***. They arrive with nests already feathered with a setting, climates, and time period, grounding our descriptions in a predetermined place. Have an image like the one in Figure 6.6 around anywhere? When we showed this picture to the fourth graders in Teena Mitchell's classroom at Charles Lake Elementary, everyone could identify. Been there. Seen that. When Sara told them that she took this picture to help her define the word

Figure 6.6 *A Real-Life Setting: Vocabulary Lesson or Fire Hazard?*

entanglement, they were intrigued. Strange word, familiar image. How could the two be married through a description?

> ***Sara:*** I explained that I had taken this picture to help me define the word *entanglement*. I further explained that descriptive writing paints a picture with words. I studied this picture in order to gather details to write my descriptive paragraph. The students agreed that what we were looking at was a mess, but mess could also describe a lot of things.
>
> ***Michael:*** We don't always write descriptions about beautiful, faraway mountain vistas—we can also describe something as everyday as coffee stains.
>
> ***Sara:*** That would be your desk with the coffee circles.
>
> ***Michael:*** I don't think anyone with that wire hazard in her office has room to talk.

After we shared the projected image with students, we put the following word description on an overhead for a shared reading. (See Appendix R for a projectable sample.)

Sample Descripton of a Thing for *Entanglement*

Beneath my desk, flanked by two lost pens, hangs an *entanglement* of wires. These brown and black wires make up the nerve center of my computer. The power strip dangles from the outlet, one end in the air and the other touching the beige carpet beside the grey computer. The wires twist and turn, braiding themselves into a mess that is almost impossible to sort or separate. Wires drop through a hole in the desk from different office machines (computer, printers, pencil sharpener, hard drive, phone, and lamp) and then snake into a ball of wires, an *entanglement* that is difficult to unravel.

As we discussed the reading, we listed some of the elements of this description: Lots of details the students identified were important—like what the wires lead to, the color of the carpet and the computer, and the fact that the mess was under a desk. A few of the girls in the class had braids in their hair and were quick to recognize the use of that verb and how it could be used to describe wires as logically as hair. We also discussed that descriptive writing includes sights, sounds, and smells and though this image didn't smell, had we chosen to write about the kitchen trash basket, smells definitely would have been part of the picture.

Teena Mitchell's is a self-contained classroom, which was in the midst of a unit on the rain forest when we paid our visit. Teeming with life, color, sounds, and smells, a rain forest was the perfect unit to reinforce strong descriptive writing. A rain forest vocabulary list is filled with things to "show, don't tell."

We began by discussing what it means to be descriptive, to write in a way that provokes the senses. This required reviewing the senses and the types of words that trigger us to think about them when we are reading a passage. We shared a sample descriptive snippet about the rain forest from one of the texts Teena had available in the classroom.

Michael: I located the example while Sara was leading the discussion of what descriptive writing involved.

Sara: This was an advantage to both of us being in the classroom.

Michael: Yes, I would suggest having your sample ready before you begin the lesson.

While reading the example we encouraged the students to cite phrases and words that created images in their minds. We then picked one of their words and created a Collaboration Cheat Sheet together with the use of an overhead projector.

Michael: I think I am still seeing spots from writing on that thing.

Sara: Occupational hazard.

We then wrote a short descriptive passage as a group, deciding that three to five sentences was a good length, using our Cheat Sheet as a guide.

We reiterated that we were not worried about beginning, middle, and end just yet—that this was a written snapshot. We divvied up the words among the class and then turned the process over to the kids. In this particular case we didn't have to suggest that they work in small groups because as soon as they had their words in hand, the bubbles of conversation floated in the room. We encouraged this chat time as they worked on the Collaboration Cheat Sheets and we walked around the room checking that the discussions were relevant to the task at hand. When the time came to write, five or so minutes into the process, some kids elected to continue in small groups while others, such as Ray, went on to write as a solo act.

Ray does a great job of describing the basic word ***snake*** in terms of what it is (reptile) and what it is not (an animal with legs) (see Figure 6.7). To do his research, he flipped to the picture of a snake in his textbook and used the glossary at the back of the book. Ray also called in for some expert testimony when he asked Michael how to describe the top of his desk. He ran the palm of his hand over the varnished surface and asked, "What's this?"

Sara: At first you answered, "It's a desk."

Michael: Yes, but it was clear Ray was searching for just the right word, so I followed up with "polished wood."

Sara: A little flash went off in Ray's eyes. You can see how he wove the simile into his writing. Not complicated words, really.

Michael: No. But just the right words for the job.

Sara: Are we going to be able to put this sample in the book? It's from fourth grade and this is a book for teachers of students in middle school and up.

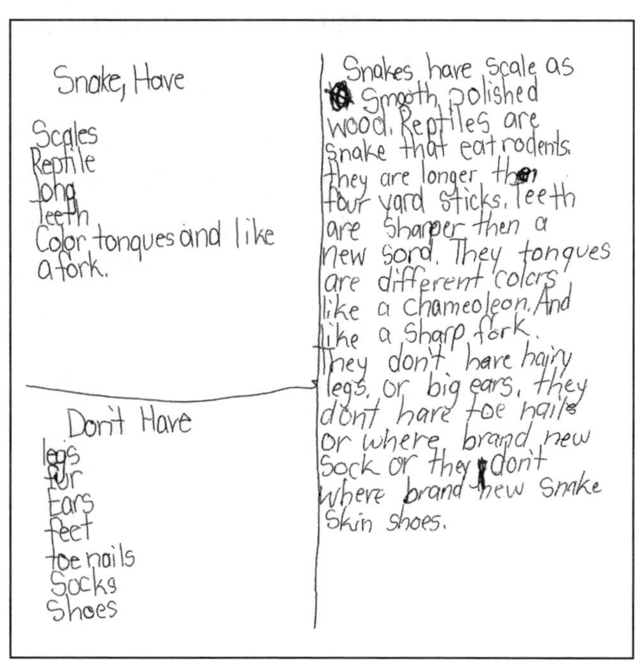

Figure 6.7 *Ray's Collaboration Cheat Sheet for* **Snake**

Michael: I hope so. I'd venture that there are more than a few middle school teachers with students in their classrooms who are writing below their grade levels.

Sara: The important thing to note is that we have found that our Collaborative Cheat Sheet works with writers in grades 1 through 12. While most of our research was done in middle school classrooms, we have seen this prewriting system work at all grade levels.

Michael: This means you can adapt it for all your students in a differentiated classroom.

A central goal of any descriptive passage, whether about a person, place, or thing, is that the portrayal should provoke the reader's senses. Instead of defining ***ruminate*** as "thinks things over," the writer could explain the clicking and whirring sound of the gears spinning in his head, coupled with the smell of smoke. We are leading students to use unfamiliar words in familiar settings, putting them into use in their own worlds.

Word Suggestions

Not only is descriptive writing perfect for depicting a person, place, or thing, it is also a great way to get to know our adjectives (see Tier Two words) a little better. Here are some Tier One and Tier Two words that should work well with this exercise. Tier Three academic words may be drawn from your content-area lessons.

Tier One: Basic Words

Easier	Harder
parrot	association
principal	tributary
jumble	enclosure
mayor	basin
shark	peninsula
banana	swindler
frog	imposter
vein	champion
channel	metropolis
island	sanctuary

Tier Two: Concept Words

Easier	Harder
fragile	reluctant
expensive	dependable
structure	tranquil
delicious	urgent
brutal	aggressive
elegant	compliant
protection	ignorant
selfish	sophisticated
evaporate	courageous
precipitation	urbane

We have found a three- to five-sentence paragraph to be a good vehicle to carry this lesson. Going beyond the single-sentence format allows the writer to add those image-evoking, sensory details that fill in the blanks for a reader. Rather than simply a list of synonyms pilfered from a thesaurus, these pieces should contain clues that allow the reader to deduce the meaning of the word. By practicing to write with specific and detailed language, the students' descriptive writing will improve along with their vocabularies.

Lesson Process

❶ **Share** one of the descriptive writing samples provided in the appendices or another of your own choosing with students by reading it out loud or copying for projection. Invite the students to name which of their senses are stirred up by the passage. This is a good time to impress that descriptive writing is not only concerned with what we see, but also what we hear, feel, taste, and smell. (Sometimes the word ***aroma*** elicits fewer giggles than ***smell***.)

❷ **Discuss** the qualities of a strong descriptive paragraph and how it should paint a picture with words. Point out that this bit of descriptive writing need not have a beginning, middle, and end as in a narrative. What we are working on might be considered a scene, snippet, or partial sketch of a larger piece. Little or no time passes; we are composing an imaginative description in a few sentences using proper paragraph form.

❸ **Model** the process by co-creating one of these word-pieces along with your students, starting with the Collaboration Cheat Sheet and scribing their suggestions on the board or projector. Ask students to identify in the sample how the word has been defined through the use of sense-evoking language. Ask the students to articulate what the word is and what it is not. Challenge the writers to come up with an image that is familiar to them and that fits the vocabulary word (such as a tangle of wires, the straight books in the library, the steam rising from the pavement).

❹ **Choose and collaborate.** Choose or assign vocabulary words (see Chapter 2, "Choosing the Words") for your writers or groups of writers to work with. Since these descriptive pieces are shorter by design, this may be an occasion where multiple words are worked on. Don't hesitate to assign duplicate words to several groups. This will promote more thoughtful discussions afterward, since many students will feel more confident contributing due to the time invested in their particular words.

❺ **Provide** vocabulary research materials for your students to use while they write. Take a look back at our ideas about Researching Words in the Digital Age (on page xi). Samples of short descriptive writing can be a constructive addition to the dictionaries, thesauruses, or handouts you have already provided. Examples could be catalogues describing products, sports magazines, or book blurbs; we have even found some image-evoking material on the back of breakfast cereal boxes.

❻ **Write.** These writing sessions need not be long drawn-out affairs—ten to fifteen minutes per word should suffice. We'll make time for revision (Version 2) later. We encourage the students to work together on the Collaboration Cheat Sheets even if they do then go on to write their short descriptive pieces solo. A bit of chatter during the collaboration and writing portion of the exercise can be expected—even so, walking around the room to gently guide errant discourse back on task is advisable.

❼ **Turn and talk.** Students take turns reading their descriptive paragraphs out loud to a person near them. Encourage peer review of the work.

❽ **Perform.** Have students present their word-pieces to the whole class. If they have been working in small groups, the whole group participates in performing their piece. Descriptive writing naturally evokes a dramatic reading. One place to find emotion in a descriptive paragraph is in the verbs. What image is evoked by the verb ***crunched***, for example? What type of inflection would enhance the word ***flutter***? Encourage your students to ham it up a bit on these and provide them a bit of rehearsal time (five minutes is plenty) in order to do so.

❾ **Assess.** Lead the class in a discussion of the writing and performance they have just experienced. Ask kids what they think the new vocabulary word means, what it doesn't mean. Does the piece appeal to the listener's senses? Did the drama displayed help to carry the meaning? Was the piece performed successful in getting the meaning across? If this is the second or third presentation of the word, how was it different from those that preceded it?

❿ **Hazards.** The writer may be tempted to spend too much time on a plot line and not enough time on careful, detailed description. Remind the writer that the definition is in the specific details included in the description and no narrative is required. A description is only a part of a story.

High Definition Through Writing Poetry

What is poetry? From those barely able to hold a pencil to scholars pursuing advanced degrees, literate and nonliterate alike have sought, through rhymes, raps, and songs, a definitive answer to Anna's question: *What is poetry?* (See Figure 7.1.)

> ***Sara:*** I once spoke at Fremd High School in Palatine, Illinois, as a warm-up act for poet Gwendolyn Brooks. She says, "Poetry is life distilled."

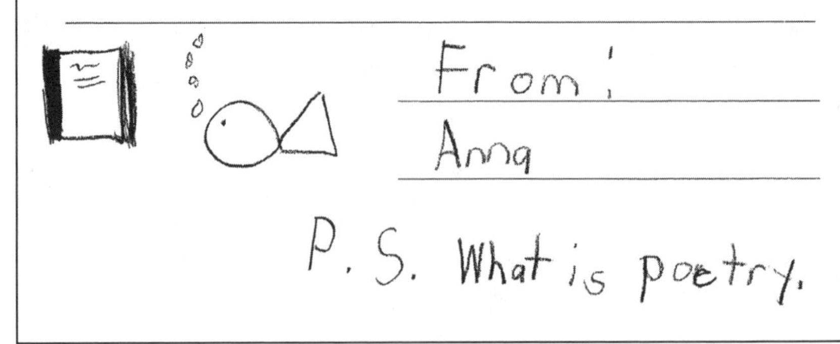

Figure 7.1 *Anna's Question:* What is poetry?

Michael: I was at the same high school a few years later and served that same role for Poet Laureate Ted Kooser, who says, "A poem is the record of a discovery, either the discovery of something in the world, or within one's self, or perhaps the discovery of something through the juxtaposition of sounds and sense within our language" (Molini and Kooser 2009).

Sara: I love this definition by Carl Sandburg: "Poetry is the shuffling of boxes of illusions buckled with a strap of facts" (Sandburg 2003).

Michael: Of course, he also said that he'd written some poetry he didn't understand himself.

Poetry—that enigmatic writing form too often put aside until all the other *important* writing is out of the way. In schools the genre is imprisoned in April or, worse, relegated to the last couple days of May when everybody's minds aren't even being brought to school anymore.

Sara: How many schools have called us over the years looking for a poet visit the last week in May, after the tests? Some even want to schedule after the grades have been submitted!

Michael: Truly an affront against the civilized world.

Sara: No kidding. Can you get any more uncivilized than the last week of school?

We believe poetry needs to be brought out of its glass case and put to work in the classroom just like other writing genres and claim its true position as creative nonfiction right beside its unabridged cousin personal narrative. Most poetry is an attempt by the author to explain what he or she thinks, sees, or believes. Precise language used to describe real events. To marginalize poetry as extra fluff to be served alongside the cupcakes at the end-of-the-year picnic deprives teachers of a versatile tool they could be using throughout the year to teach all the language arts standards *and* vocabulary to boot.

Sara: This is a natural fit—so much poetry is an author's attempt at defining something.

Michel: Right, what are metaphors and similes but definitions in Sunday go-to-meeting clothes?

Sara: Emily said, "Hope is the thing with feathers . . ."

Michael: Yeah, tell that to a Thanksgiving turkey.

We know that a lot of excellent teachers worry about assessment when it comes to poetry. Exactly how are they supposed to assign a score to a piece about their student's love of a grandparent or one making a case against the oppression of a minority group?

Sara: Simply put, one doesn't.

Michael: Are you saying that we just write poetry for the sheer enjoyment of it and to heck with the lesson plans?

Sara: You know me better than that.

Michael: I know but it's my job to ask the leading questions in this book.

Writing Vocabulary Poems

I've Been in Verse Situations

For any lesson plan to be successful it must have an objective. We made the case for using poetry to teach the language arts standards in Sara's book *Practical Poetry* and in our book *Outspoken!* Here we would like to extend the genre's utility to vocabulary acquisition. Therefore, we urge teachers to keep in mind their classroom goals in assessing students' definition poetry. If the goal of the teacher's lesson is that students should come away with a deeper understanding of the meanings of words from a unit about the feudal system or *To Kill a Mockingbird*, the assessment should focus on the students' ability to meet that objective.

Sara: In other words, don't lay too much pressure on every little poem.

Michael: In the case of a vocabulary poem, the written piece is not merely an artifact, but is in itself an assessment of the students' word knowledge.

When we first started to visit classrooms to focus on vocabulary development through student collaboration, writing, and performance, we began with poetry, because that's the genre in which we are most fluent. Poetry is a great form to use to teach new vocabulary, it encourages thoughtful comparison, naturally incorporates a variety of patterns, and is short with flexible rules.

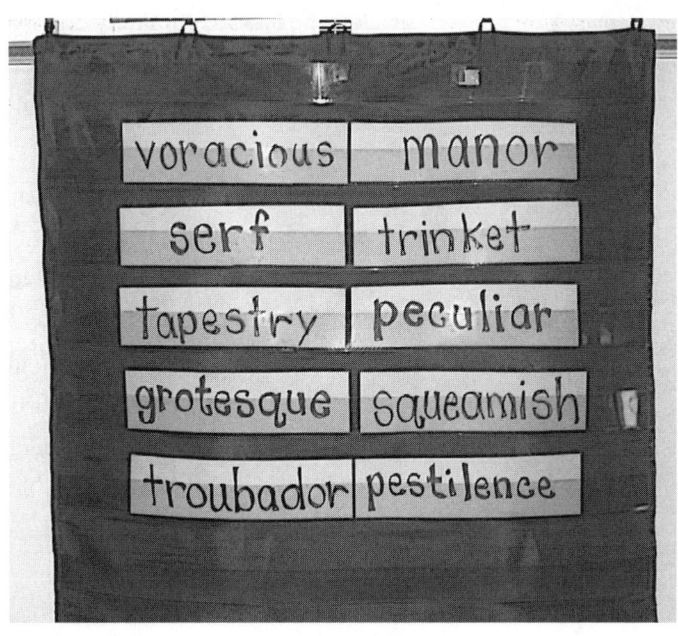

Figure 7.2 *Sixth-Grade Vocabulary Words from Unit on the Feudal System*

Poetry is especially effective with English language learners. According to Dr. Nancy Johnson, a professor of English/language arts and children's literature at Western Washington University, "When we are learning a new language aren't we actually speaking poetry?" (2009). She cites a passage in Kathy Applegate's novel *Home of the Brave* as an example. The protagonist, Kek, a recent immigrant from the Sudan, "uses metaphor as he seeks to name something in English that he doesn't have the definitive term for as he tries to explain an idea or an object or even a feeling. For example, when his plane lands in Minnesota at the very beginning of the book, he experiences snow for the first time and someone asks him 'Do you like the cold?' His response is: 'I want to say / No; this cold is like claws on my skin!' Then a tiny bit later he comments: 'The man gives me a fat shirt / and soft things like hands.' And later: 'I am a tall boy / like all my people. / My arms stick out of the coat like lonely trees. / My fingers cannot make the gloves work. / I shake my head. / I say, This American is hard work. / His laughter makes little clouds.'"

Sometimes the great expanse of a blank page can be a bit daunting for our second language learners. The fact that most poems are shorter makes the lesson ultimately doable for a student who is still acquiring the new language. Add to this the fact that poetry encourages the type of word stretching that is done by many language learners and this quickly adds up to success. The piece in Figure 7.3 was written by three boys, Saiid, Roman, and Demitri, in a seventh-grade ELL class at Rabat American School in Morocco. English was at least the third language that these boys were acquiring and each spoke a different native tongue. There are not too many MFA creative writing students who would not be proud of this piece.

English language learners and just plain language learners often reach for apt comparisons to substitute for unknown words, making them natural poets. We wrote with students in the third through twelfth grades in language arts, math, social studies, and science classes and found that

Figure 7.3 Isolation *Poem*

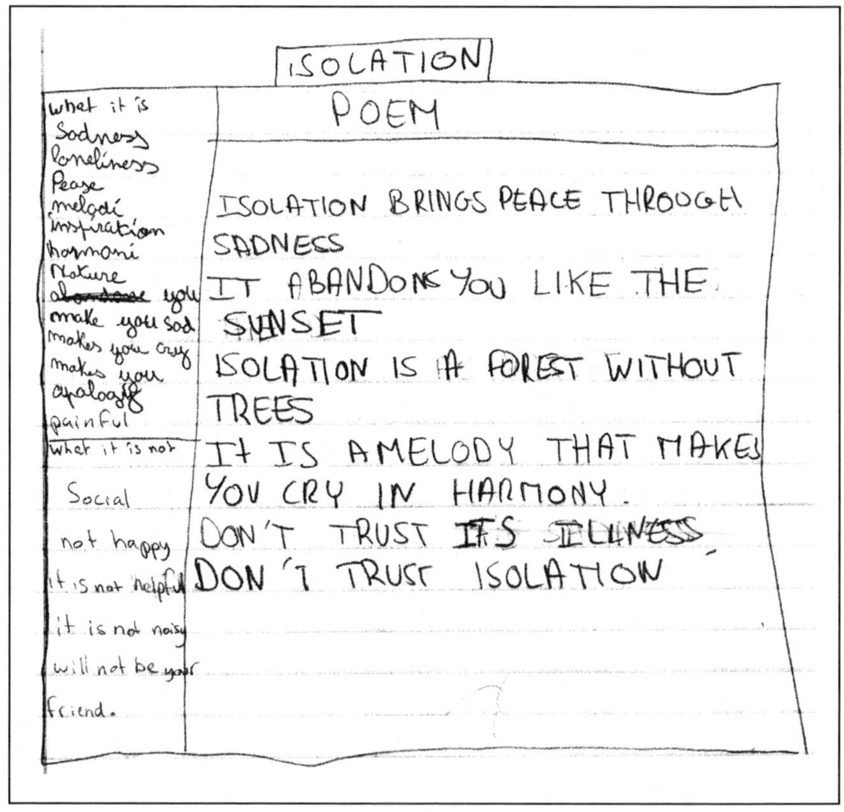

ISOLATION
POEM

what it is
Sadness
loneliness
Pease
melodi
inspiration
harmoni
Nature
~~abandone~~ you
make you sad
makes you cry
makes you
apalogy
painful
what it is not
Social
not happy
it is not helpful
it is not noisy
will not be your
friend.

ISOLATION BRINGS PEACE THROUGH
SADNESS
IT ABANDONS YOU LIKE THE
SUNSET
ISOLATION IS A FOREST WITHOUT
TREES
IT IS AMELODY THAT MAKES
YOU CRY IN HARMONY.
DON'T TRUST ~~ITS SILLINESS~~
DON'T TRUST ISOLATION

poetry had a place in word study in all classrooms. Poetry writing and performing naturally scaffolds to the student's ability, stresses the good communication techniques of being concise and precise, and instigates deeper thinking.

Robbie Tupa and Angela Randjelovic's sixth-grade social studies classrooms at Bay Village Middle schools were among our first visits. They were in the midst of a unit on the feudal system and had identified unfamiliar words before our arrival. We wrote the words on slips of paper and the students partnered up and drew them out of a basket. We settled on this system after a frustrating writing lesson in math (see Chapter 5, "Narrative Writing") where we let students choose from the list on the board and where, in one class, 99 percent of them chose the word *random*, thereby tanking our classroom vocabulary objectives. Live and learn.

We began the lesson by sharing a couple of our own definition poems with the class (see Appendices S, T, U, and V for projectable samples).

Subtle

Subtle
isn't a punch in the nose,
a kick in the shins,
a bee in the toes.

Subtle
stays quiet,
yet
everyone knows.

Sara Holbrook (1996)

Redundant

Redundant.
Redundant.
Quit kicking my desk.
Redundant.
Redundant.
Please stop.
You're a pest.
Redundant.
Redundant.
You said that before.
Redundant.
Redundant.
Redundant.
NO MORE!

Sara Holbrook (2010)

Novice hasn't quite figured things out yet
you see he's just been sent into the game
doesn't have much experience
but he's more than willing to try just the same
it's not his fault, everyone has to start
somewhere at sometime
and I'm sure he's gonna
get the hang of things
I'm just saying . . . I'm glad he's your surgeon
and not mine.

Michael Salinger (2009)

Reiterate you can say that again!
and she will
sometimes re-phrased sometimes
verbatim
but the message remains the same
for you see, reiterate conceives
that once is never enough
to get her message across
it's pretty tough competing
with all the noise of this busy world
so, she believes
a notion worth saying
is also worth repeating

Michael Salinger (2009)

As always, the next step was to model the lesson with a group write. We left a sample on the board as a reference point for the students when they moved on to their own writing. The word we chose was to work with was ***nobility***. In fact, this was so early in our classroom use of this writing activity that we had yet to fully develop our pattern for prewriting!

That nobleman's a fancy pants.
He is rich and fat.
He lives in a castle.
No togas, no jeans.
He wears velvet robes
and lace on his sleeves.

The students' ideas were image rich and based on their study in and beyond the textbook. Notice the nobleman did not wear a toga—an observation that seems slightly more relevant if you consider that the classes had just completed a unit on ancient worlds. The students were accessing their prior knowledge as they worked together to discover meaning in the new vocabulary. As is always the case, a lively classroom discussion drove the brainstorm, how noblemen had stained glass windows in their castles while the serfs lived in huts made of mud, straw, and manure, providing Angela and Robbie multiple opportunities to reteach details about the unit.

The students then broke into pairs and small groups to discuss their words. After the initial collaboration with a partner, Taylor elected to write on her own. Taylor wrote a detailed poem defining ***squeamish***, a word not exclusively connected to the feudal system but one that had cropped up in the unit in relation to the plague. Taylor is a very conscientious student, which you can see reflected in her careful prewrite (see Figure 7.4)—how she meticulously checked off the details of what *squeamish* is and is not as she developed her lyrical poem. We let students know that it was okay to rhyme or not rhyme, but this being sixth grade, many students chose a rhyming pattern for their poem.

Chris and Jillian worked together to produce their poem about the more subject-specific term ***serf*** (Figure 7.5). Although their poem is not as ornate, it certainly evidences that the writers understood the concept of what it means to be a *serf* and how that term differs from a slave because a *serf* is "bound to the land." Since our objective was that the poems should reflect the writers' knowledge of the meaning of the words they were defining through their poetry, Taylor, Jillian, and Chris all fulfilled the assignment. Concentrating the focus of our lesson on word meaning makes assessment more straightforward. Our main criterion for success is, does the student understand the new vocabulary word?

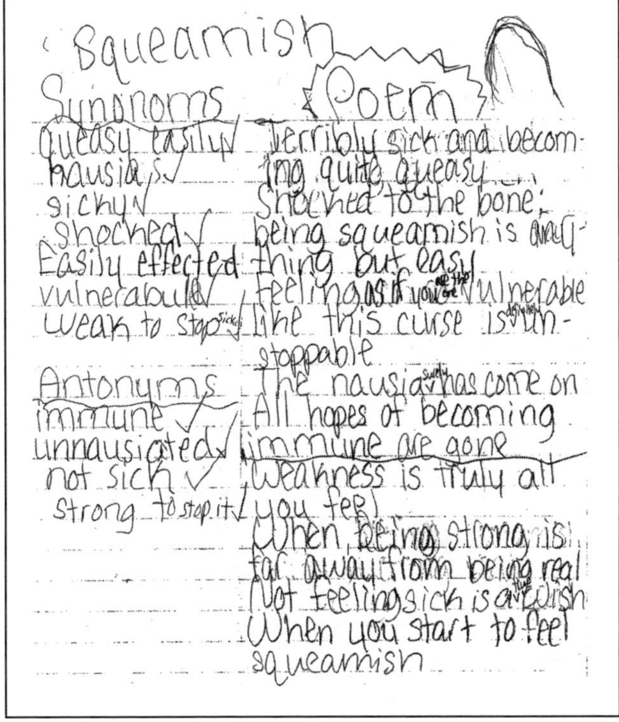
Squeamish

Synonoms
queasy easily
nausia
sicky
shocked
Easily effected
vulnerabul
weak to stop

Antonyms
immune
unnausiated
not sick
strong to stop it

Poem
Terribly sick and becom-
ing quite queasy
Shocked to the bone;
being squeamish is a
thing but easy
Feeling as if you vulnerable
like this curse is un-
stoppable
The nausia has come on
All hopes of becoming
immune are gone
Weakness is truly all
you feel
When being strong is
far away from being real
Not feeling sick is a wish
When you start to feel
squeamish

Figure 7.4 *Taylor's Prewrite for* **Squeamish**

Following the writing portion of the lesson, students rehearsed their poems aloud in small groups and then took turns presenting to the class. After each student presentation, we took the opportunity to discuss the word's meaning again.

Any time you bring the arts into the classroom, in this case by introducing new words through poetry, be prepared to be often pleased and occasionally awed by the students' improvisation. Some will create a piece of art that will astound you. The objective of our lesson was simply for students to expand their word knowledge, but look at what

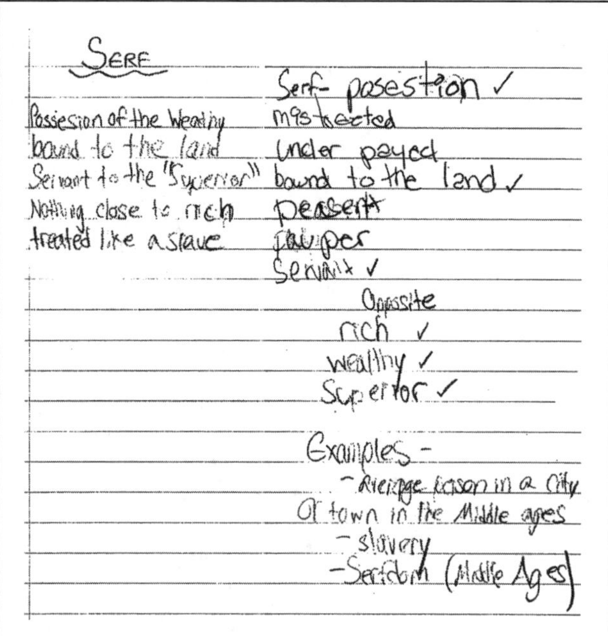

Serf

Serf- posestion ✓

Possesion of the Wealthy — mistreated

bound to the land — under payed

Servant to the "Superior" — bound to the land ✓

Nothing close to rich — peasent

treated like a slave — pauper

Servant ✓

Opposite

rich ✓

wealthy ✓

Superior ✓

Examples -

- Average person in a City Or town in the Middle ages

- slavery

- Serfdom (Middle Ages)

Figure 7.5 *Chris and Jillian's Prewrite for* **Serf**

Figure 7.6 *Performance Shares the Learning*

came out of Sarah and Maranda's collaboration on the word ***tapestry*** (see Figure 7.7). Beyond the beautiful poem, look at all the details about tapestries that the girls discussed. Even though words like ***fabric*** and ***carpet*** did not wind up in the final poem, we can see that those details were part of the discussion, becoming interwoven into the writers' knowledge of the word *tapestry*. The writers understood that poetry is distilled language and prioritized the information they collected while deciding what would end up in their final piece. This type of higher-order thinking strategy can be carried over into all their reading and writing.

During the performance part of the lesson, we were able to hear another poem on the word *tapestry*, written by Katie (Figure 7.8). Following the presentation of these poems, we discussed what each brought to the meaning of the word *tapestry*, thereby reinforcing the word meaning with the rest of the class.

In contrast to Sarah and Maranda's poem, Katie's poem is typical of many middle school writers who bend and twist logic to try and fit their ideas into a rhyming pattern with awkward results. Had we had more time with this class, we would have suggested a Version 2 of this poem for Katie, and asked her to pick out the most important ideas and lose the rhyme scheme just to see how that feels. We always let kids know

Tapestry	
stories	The Tapestry's Waves
cloth	
lively dancing lyrics	Lively dancing figures
unraveling the ribbons	Singing us their song
woven pictures	Unraveling the ribbons
weave	Of the woven pictures
hanging on walls	Drenching our smelly memories
pictures and designs	Stuck-up in this squeaky-clean
fabric	World
covering	A story without a cover
carpet	
furniture	
art	
fighting my mind	
Not	
not a sclupture	
not a book yet a	
story	

Figure 7.7 *Sarah and Maranda's Collaboration on* **Tapestry**

Tapestry

fabric	pictures, designs, a woven delight
pictures	
designes	the people who made it
wove	put up a good fight
hung on walls	
cover furniture	Its large and its tall
describe a story	
rug	[illegible]
moside	It'll hang on your wall
weaving	
montage	A fabric that can certainly say it all
representation	
not just an	A huge mosiac representation
ordinary piece	
of fabric	It'll give your guests a good presentation
	When weaving and winding
	your head will grinding
	It can be anything you'll soon be finding

Figure 7.8 *Katie's* **Tapestry** *Poem*

that they own both Version 1 and Version 2 and ultimately get to choose which is working better for them. Rhyming is still popular with this age group, and they are totally delighted with themselves if they can "make it rhyme." What we want to do is build on the quality and content of their writing without quashing that delight. Some of these middle schoolers are still toting stuffed animals in their backpacks. It's a growing process. We want to help them find their voices, not simply cut them off at the knuckles by saying rhyming poems are intrinsically bad. That's like pressing delete on the delight factor for many middle school kids!

Pattern in Poetry

There's Method in His Madness

Of course, rhyming is just one of the patterns of poetry. All told, there are at least a gazillion different patterns (by exact count).

From lists to limericks, from sonnets, to rap—patterns are part of what often helps define poetry across the centuries and among all cultures.

Vacillate cannot
make up its mind, up or down,
stay or wait—who cares?

Sara Holbrook (2005)

Patterns, such as this haiku, can be part of what scares people away from creating poetry. Don't know the rules for a sonnet? Worried that you will get mired in a quatrain quagmire? Here's a hint from a couple of veteran poets: If you don't know all the rules of poetry patterns, make one up! Seriously. Let the kids make them up. If there is anything more boring than a dreary vocabulary lesson, it's an afternoon counting downbeats while analyzing the structure of a poem. Don't go there!

That said, following a simple pattern may be just the ticket for making the definition poem memorable. Here is a line pattern we made up: True, true, false, true, rhyme. We took that pattern into Mark Kevesdy's sixth-grade math classroom (where they often study patterns) and worked together to write this poem about equilateral triangles:

Each angle has 60 degrees
It has three sides
It does not have four sides
All angles equal 180 degrees
A triangle does not have knees.

Do we care if a triangle has knees? Of course not, but does this help make the rest of the poem (and the rules about equilateral triangles) more memorable? Yes! Encourage kids to make up patterns, copy other patterns, use the poems throughout this chapter as mentor texts, or choose no pattern at all. Just put poetry to work. We are writing poetry to help with word knowledge, using poetry as a vehicle for learning.

In Libby Royko's eighth-grade class we were working from a list of unknown words that students had chosen from reading *To Kill a*

Mockingbird. As we mentioned in Chapter 2, the list of unknown words was extensive, filling two entire blocks of her three-section blackboard. Libby told us that she likes to give students a heads-up on some of the difficult words in advance, a few words from each chapter that she predicts might trip them up and delay their enjoyment of the story. When introducing a word, she generally asks the students what they think the word means as a way of kicking off the discussion and affording her an opportunity to reinforce root-recognition strategies she has taught. Hers is an inclusion classroom, and reading Harper Lee's novel *To Kill a Mockingbird* is a requirement for all eighth graders. Libby explained that preteaching helps keep her students from becoming overwhelmed by unfamiliar terms and giving up on the text. For the purposes of our writing exercises, students helped choose words

Figure 7.9 *Eighth-Grade Student (Hopefully) No Longer* **Perplexed**

that they were interested in for further study, such as: ***baffled***, ***malevolent***, ***nocturnal***, ***compelled***, ***benevolence***, ***morbid***, ***excessive***, ***perplexed***, and ***peril***. Libby had dictionaries and thesauruses handy for student research. That, in addition to teaching and peer support, made the brainstorming and writing flow smoothly.

We began as we always do with a shared reading of a definition poem (see Appendix S, T, U, and V for projectable samples).

Julianne and Brittney began their writing as a pair, discussing the word, looking it up, and writing down what the word *baffled* means and what it does not mean.

You can see that they have almost identical Collaborative Cheat Sheets. But they had different ideas as the writing progressed, causing Brittney to take off in her own direction in what she labels Poem 2 on her paper. "Is that okay?" they wanted to know. "Can we write our own poems?" YES! (See Figures 7.10a and 7.10b.)

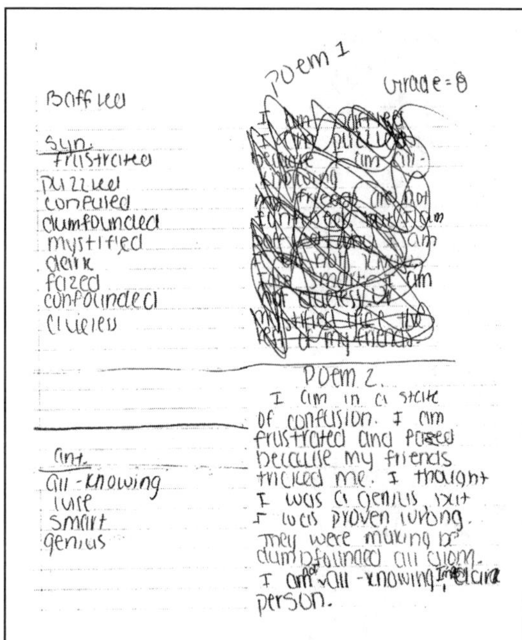

Baffled

syn.
frustrated
puzzled
confused
dumfounded
mystified
dark
fazed
confounded
clueless

ant.
all-knowing
wise
smart
genius

Poem 1

Grade = 8

Poem 2

I am in a state of confusion. I am frustrated and fazed because my friends tricked me. I thought I was a genius, but I was proven wrong. They were making be dumbfounded all along. I am not all-knowing, I'm a clueless person.

Figure 7.10a *Brittney's* **Baffled** *Poem*

Baffled

synonyms:
frustrated
puzzled
confused
dumbfounded
mystified
fazed
confounded
clueless

antonyms:
all knowing
wise
smart
genius

I am Baffled
I'm puzzled because
I am not all knowing
my friends are not
confused, but I am
Baffled, why I am
I do not know
I am not smart, I
am dumbfounded
~~I am cof~~
I am fazed because
I did not think, I did
not imagine of what
the day would bring
me, I am now not
wise, but mystified

Figure 7.10b *Julianne's* **Baffled** *Poem*

Having already benefited from the prewrite discussion, both girls were able to marry the word ***baffled*** with their own concrete (not baffling at all) examples.

Poetry is a genre that we have taught at all grade levels, so as our excitement about writing definition poems grew, we began to stretch, trying out strategies in grades 3 through 12 to see what kinds of adjustments we might need to make in order to adapt the writing lesson for different age groups.

Michael: I can't think of any adjustments, can you?

Sara: Well, the third graders' desktops are a bit lower.

Was the quality of the writing different at the high school level than it was in the third grade? Sure. But the value and simplicity of the lessons were effective in each and every classroom where we worked. Remember Ben from Chapter 1? Born into a writing family, Ben's vocabulary development has been a group project since his birth. Ben was in Mrs. Renee Voce's third-grade classroom at Emerick Elementary in Purcellville, Virginia, when Sara visited for a lesson in writing definition poems. She let Renee know that this was the first time she had tried this writing strategy with third graders. Together, Renee and Sara put that week's vocabulary list on slips of paper for the students to randomly choose. Sara shared a definition poem aloud (Appendix T) and then led the class in a group write on the board. Everyone then pulled out their writer's notebooks and paired up for discussion, using dictionaries for reference.

Renee and Sara circulated as some of the students wrote in pairs and some (including Ben)

I am in a state of confusion.
I am frustrated and fazed
because my friends
tricked me. I thought
I was a genius, but
I was proven wrong.
They were making me
dumbfounded all along.
I am not all-knowing,
I'm a dark person.

Brittney, Grade 8

I am baffled
I'm puzzled because
I am not all knowing
My friends are not
confused, but I am
Baffled. Why I am
I do not know
I am not smart, I
am dumbfounded
I am fazed because
I did not think, I did
not imagine of what
the day would bring
me. I am now not wise,
but mystified.

Julianne, Grade 8

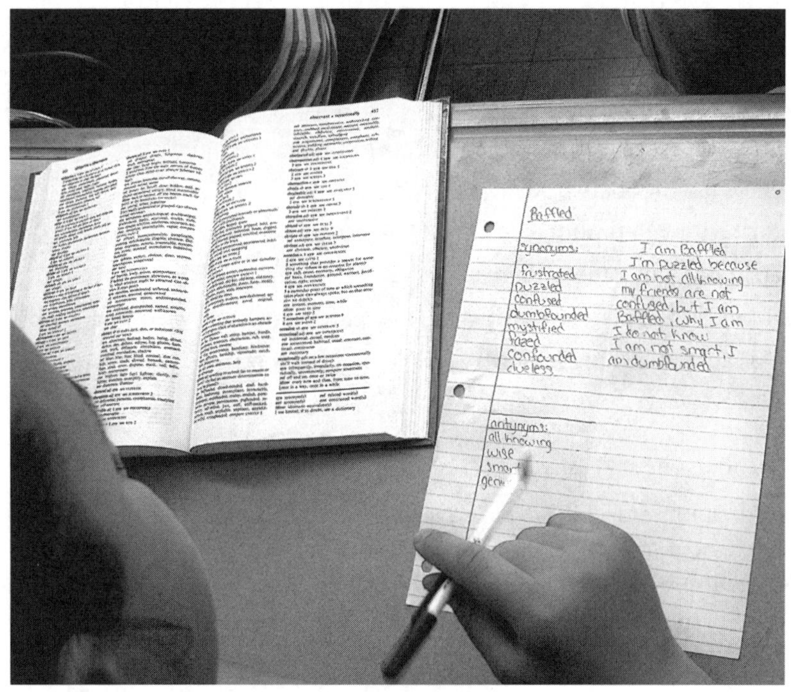

Figure 7.11 *Writing with Research Tools*

Figure 7.12 *Ben's Poem Defining* **Swirl**

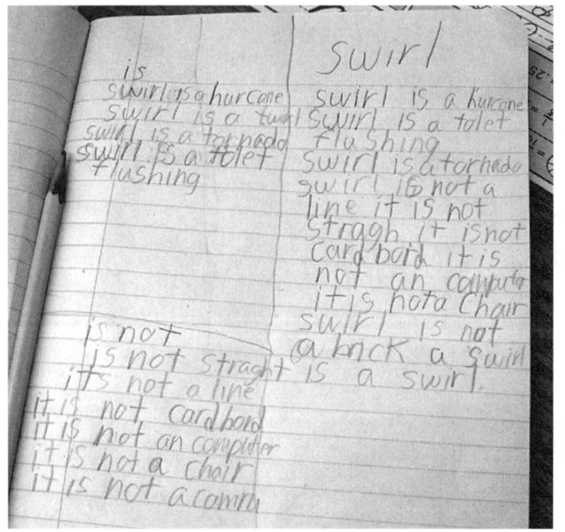

chose to write on their own after their initial brainstorming collaboration with their partner. At Emerick, teachers are mandated to teach a list of vocabulary words each week that are not related to the students' units of study. Renee was impressed with how well her students did with this new activity, and with how seamlessly the vocabulary lesson dovetailed into her writing objectives.

When students write poetry about words, they also wind up writing about their lives. In Donna Kohn's tenth-grade class at Mentor High School, Mentor, Ohio, the students were reading *Lord of the Flies*. Here again, early into the novel, the list of unfamiliar words was extensive. Donna had distributed a list of challenge words to her students along with short definitions, acknowledging that the list proved to be little more than a crib sheet for students during their reading. She didn't expect that her students would necessarily be able to apply these words in their conversations or subsequent writing. Among the words were ***cordoned***, ***belligerent***, ***torrid***, ***derision***,

perilous, ***myopia***, ***ululation***, and ***abyss***. Mostly, Donna wanted to provide them with a reading aid in their fluent enjoyment of the text. As was the case in Libby's eighth-grade classroom, this was a novel that was a requisite for that grade level. The word that the students chose for the modeling session was ***distended***.

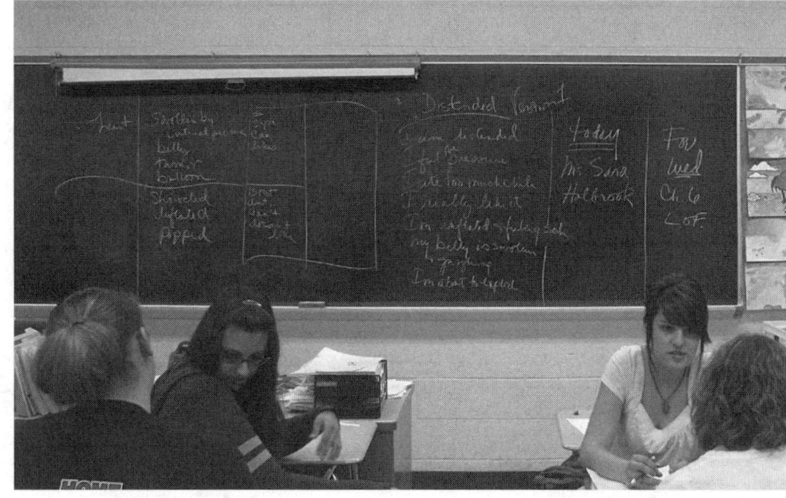

Figure 7.13 *Tenth-Grade Classroom Group Write,* **Distended**

I am distended
I feel the pressure
I ate too much chili
I really like it.
I'm inflated and feeling sick.
My belly is swollen and gurgling.
I'm about to explode.

Revision Writing

Less Is More—More or Less

One thing that we did do differently at the tenth-grade level than we did at the elementary level was to put a greater emphasis on the fact that we would be writing two versions of the poem, time permitting (as guest artists, we rarely are able to extend our lessons over more than one day). After we wrote Version 1 (see the poem for *distended*) we did not take the time to do a revision, but discussed the fact that this draft had way too many "I"s in it, something we could fix in a subsequent draft. Students then turned to discuss the words they had pulled.

Is	nearsightedness
Syn	ignorant
Can	
likes	things only concerning themself
Isn't	
Ant	observant
Can't	
Dislike	World news

Myopia Version 1
We are myopia.
Without care of others.
While focusing on ourselves,
we forget all else.
We are nearsighted and
ignorant, and not observant
or caring.
So don't bug us with World
news or the danger the Earth is in.
We don't care.

Myopia Version 2
We are myopic,
without care of others.
While focusing on ourselves,
we tend to forget all else.
Nearsighted and ignorant, we
are not observant or caring.
So don't bother telling us
what is happening elsewhere.
We don't care.

Figure 7.14 *Brittany's Version 1 and Version 2*

Brittany wanted to know, "Is it okay if I change the word a little in my Version 2?" She wanted to change *myopia* to ***myopic*** to make her poem work better after thinking and talking about the word (Figure 7.14). YES! This is a wonderful way for students to actually handle words, to turn them over and examine possible twists and turns in various applications.

We suggested to the students that they may even choose to change the point of view in their Version 2, and Melanie and Amy took us up on that in their poem defining *derision* (see Figure 7.15). The writing from these students was fun to read and occasionally stunning.

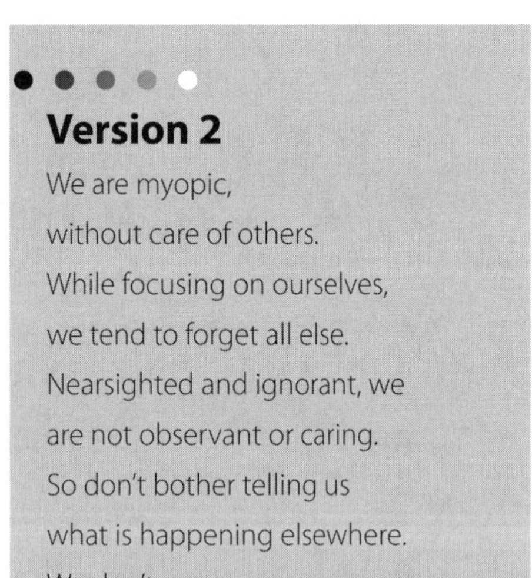

Version 2

We are myopic,
without care of others.
While focusing on ourselves,
we tend to forget all else.
Nearsighted and ignorant, we
are not observant or caring.
So don't bother telling us
what is happening elsewhere.
We don't care.

Brittany, Grade 10

Belligerent: I am full of rage and walking trouble.

Festooned: My clothes are covered in rhinestones, I wear pink high heels.

Torrid: I boil. I burn. I scorch and I flame.

Abyss: I am the abyss / Endless / Cannot stop / forever unbound.

Officious became a bossy Boy Scout, *Ebullience* a cheerleader, and *Festooned* declined to be Amish or a pilgrim, each poem evidence that the writers could see applications for these words outside of the novel and useable in their own worlds.

But perhaps the most striking example came from a football player who wants to be known simply as McKnight. By all appearances (his posture, his stare, his limited discussion, his prewrite, his shoelaces), he just wasn't that into the whole concept of writing poetry. Not surprisingly, he didn't attempt a Version 2, either. No need really. He had said it all in Version 1, leaving little doubt that he knew exactly what it meant to be ***cordoned*** (see Figure 7.16). Not cordoned as it was used in the book. Cordoned for real.

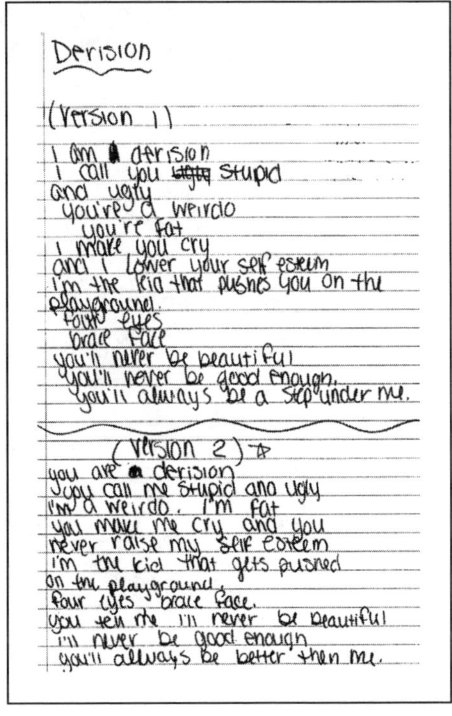
Derision

(Version 1)

I am derision
I call you stupid
and ugly
you're a weirdo
you're fat
I make you cry
and I lower your self esteem
I'm the kid that pushes you on the playground.
Four eyes
brace face
you'll never be beautiful
you'll never be good enough.
you'll always be a step under me.

(Version 2)

you are derision
you call me stupid and ugly
I'm a weirdo. I'm fat
you make me cry and you never raise my self esteem
I'm the kid that gets pushed on the playground.
four eyes brace face.
you tell me I'll never be beautiful
I'll never be good enough
you'll always be better then me.

Figure 7.15 *Melanie and Amy's* **Derision** *Poem*

> Something's holding me back
> I am cordoned by my peers
> they tell me what to do
> I can't be independent
> If I do they make fun of me
> They tease me and I comply.

McKnight took this new vocabulary word and applied it to his own life experiences, his own perception of where he fit in his high school hierarchal world. Like any good poet, his work was thoughtful and personal, an outward expression of an internal concept. He's taken the word *cordoned* and claimed ownership.

Figure 7.16 *McKnight's* **Cordoned** *Poem*

restricts you
Boundaries

Somethings holding me back
I am cordend by my peers
they tell me what to do
I cant be independent
If I Do they make fun of me
They tease me and I comply

Not open spaces
Not No limits

Sara: Are we imparting too much meaning on this little definition poem?

Michael: I don't know; let me tell you about this little red wheelbarrow . . .

Tier One: Basic Words

Easier	*Harder*
tragedy	calamity
trade	barter
corridor	arcade
void	abyss
envy	covet
assembly	parliament
avoid	inescapable
imposter	fraud
larynx	predecessor
opossum	expedite

Tier Two: Conceptual Words

Easier	*Harder*
consume	ingest
excel	surpass
sturdy	durable
lax	superficial
strenuous	fervent
bulk	preponderance
recess	respite
imitation	synthetic
plunge	immerse
plentiful	abundant
abstract	obtuse

Lesson Process

❶ **Share** one of the definition poem samples provided in the appendices (Appendices S, T, U, V) or another of your own choosing by reading it out loud or projecting a copy for your students. Poets by nature are in the business of marrying concepts and words. What is a metaphor other than a shorthand attempt at definition?

❷ **Discuss** the qualities specific to the poem. Is there a refrain, alliteration, or pattern? Highlight the concept of poetry being concise and precise—a novel may be compared to a feature film while a poem is more like a snapshot. You may want to talk about the importance of patterns and form in poetry, or you may want to rely on the students' prior knowledge and just let them choose their own approach. You may want to list some of the most common forms. What forms do the students already know? Have you made up a new form of your own? This is can be an opportunity to reinforce the elements of poetry, but leave the door open to let students experiment.

❸ **Model** the process by collaboratively writing a definition poem for one of the vocabulary words you are teaching on the board with the class. Use the Collaboration Cheat Sheet (Appendix A) for your brainstorm session.

> ***Michael:*** I like to model using a simple set pattern already in mind so that the students have a clear outline with a definite ending to follow. (Don't feel guilty about choosing a word you feel will work well with the exercise.)

Sara: I like to start with free verse. This is to say, there is no right or wrong approach.

Michael: But both of us title our model poem the same.

Sara: Yep. Version 1. Don't linger too long talking about revisions at this modeling stage, just hint that we know we are not crafting a final draft.

Later, the students can graduate to more complex forms or even make up patterns of their own. Leave this sample piece in view for the students when they work on their own.

❹ **Choose and collaborate.** Put your students in small groups of two to four. Have them choose (or you may wish to assign) vocabulary words (see Chapter 2, "Choosing the Words") for your writers or groups of writers. If you have a list of perhaps ten words you would like the students to master, you will want to make sure that each word gets chosen by at least one writing group. Since poetry is meant to be snapshot writing and consequently short, this genre lends itself to the assigning of several words per working group. For example, if you were writing a definition haiku, four words per group of collaborators would not be too much.

❺ **Provide** vocabulary research materials for your students. Ideally this should not be limited to a classroom set of dictionaries. Take a look back at our ideas about Researching Words in the Digital Age (on page xi). Use glossaries, handouts, thesauruses, and websites to find examples of the word being used in different contexts. Adding a rhyming dictionary to the mix could come in handy. If you are in the midst of a unit on poetry, you might even want to roll in a cart of poetry books from the library for the kids' review.

❻ **Write.** Provide writing time in class. Remind your students to utilize the Collaboration Cheat Sheet to organize their group brainstorms. In instances where each writing group is working on more than one word, it is helpful to instruct the students to finish all their prewrites before moving on to write their poem. When the students do move on to write their poems, they may decide to write them all as collaborative pieces or divvy them up among their members. Whether the students elect to write independently or as a group, it is most important that the collaboration take place during the brainstorming portion.

❼ **Turn and talk.** Have students share their poems out loud within their groups. This provides an opportunity for first edits and informal peer review preparing the students to present their poems in front of the rest of the class. Poetry often relies on rhythm. Reading out loud gives the opportunity to test the pieces for "flow." If your students find that their poems have rough spots when read out loud, this is an indication that the work needs to be revised on the page.

❽ **Perform.** Invite students to present their word-pieces to the whole class. If they have been working in small groups, each member of the group needs to have a role in performing their piece. Poetry naturally lends itself to performance. We believe a poem doesn't truly exist until it has been read aloud to another person.

❾ **Assess.** Lead the class in a discussion of the writing and performance they have just experienced. Ask kids what they think the new vocabulary word means and what it doesn't mean. We are not judging the poems as to which is best, but seeking to find a complete definition of the word. How does each poem add to our understanding of the word? Was the piece precise and concise?

10 Hazards. If an initial pattern is used in modeling a definition poem, it should be simple such as the true, true, false, true, rhyme pattern mentioned in this chapter. Trying to write perfect iambic pentameter or a villanelle right out of the starting block can elevate the form over the content. Crafting a pattern or form is not the final goal of this exercise. We want any pattern we use to be an aid to our writers' understanding of the new vocabulary.

11 Extra credit. This genre fits well into an anthology format. Have your students collect their work and create a book. Illustrations to augment the poems are another opportunity to ingrain the meaning of the new words.

High Definition Through
Big Words

Racism. Peace. Freedom. Democracy. Education. These are Big Words. On one hand, easy enough to affix with a face value meaning, but simultaneously too complex and resonant to be bound by only one definition. These words may not be long, obscure words, not even necessarily multisyllabic, compounded, academic-challenge-type words. Big Words are characterized by often lifelong efforts of people to harvest definitions out of daily existence and then putting them into jars for others to sample and compare. Like barbeque sauce, there is rarely one best winner and unlike skunks, Big Words are not black and white.

Big Words are ***purple*** or ***aqua***, unique blends of other Big Words like ***fear*** and ***love***.

Sara: All you need is love.

Michael: According to the J. Geils band, love stinks.

Sara: Love is a warm puppy. It's never having to say you're sorry. It's on its way . . .

Michael: Love is a battlefield.

Some words are living dichotomies. In his movie *Love and Death*, Woody Allen wrote, "To love is to suffer. To avoid suffering one must not love. But then one suffers from not loving. Therefore, to love is to suffer; not to love is to suffer; to suffer is to suffer. To be happy is to love. To be happy, then, is to suffer, but suffering makes one unhappy. Therefore, to be unhappy, one must love or love to suffer or suffer from too much happiness. I hope you're getting this down."

What we are truly getting while listening to Allen's onscreen character is not only a good laugh but an example of just how tough it is to corral a Big Word with a definition. But this is where we often find ourselves in our classrooms when we are called upon to ask our students to contemplate life on a more philosophical level. Whether discussing the word *prejudice* in conjunction with a unit on civil rights or introducing the term *empathy* as part of addressing the school's antibullying policy, helping students wrap their arms around these weighty words can be heavy lifting.

Words can be helpful or hurtful in relationships—relationships among friends, families, and countries. Even some of the simplest Big Words have different connotations among different demographic groups. Ask a group of kids to define *fight*, for example, and the boys will describe an altercation involving fists or weapons, but the girls are more likely to reference eye rolls and shunning. Taking time to have students define *peace*, *war*, *compromise*, or *resolution* and all the nuances that lie between can help supplement your schools' efforts to combat bullying.

The Mentor Text

What's the Big Idea?

Unfortunately, some of our students' most sincere attempts to define Big Words through nonfiction essays and poems are not nearly as funny or original as Mr. Allen's treatise on love. Often veering into triteness, euphemisms, and clichés, their efforts can miss the mark because they lack concrete examples. Love may not always be suffering, but it is a whole lot more than "just having someone's back" (where? when? does that mean listening to them rant or telling them what to do?). Any of the exercises demonstrated in this book can be used to help students define these concept words—poems, letters, diary entries. In addition to those examples, we want to add one more idea—to help kids hop over the shallow streams of media runoff when laying claim to these Big Words, we believe it is time well spent rewriting a piece of mentor text.

Mentor texts provide a framework that allows the students to get to the meat of the work with a bit of built-in support. Very few of us are sent down the driveway on our first two-wheeler foray without the aid of training wheels. There's so much going on—pedaling, steering, the dog barking, a coiled garden hose, little brothers running in circles, and the woodpile—all conspiring to knock us from our precarious perch, that a little extra bit of a prop is warranted.

Michael: I wish someone had told that to my dad.

Similarly, when asking our students to tackle the meaning of Big Words it is useful to provide an example for them to follow. This not only helps steer them in the right direction, it enhances the likelihood of their success. Like training wheels, these crutches will disappear, as our students get more comfortable with the concepts they are tackling. Here is a simple example, the mentor text being a short introduction of a cautionary narrative on keeping wild animals as pets.

> Wild animals are at home in jungles, swamps, and open plains. But some wild animals live in zoos. Some even live in people's homes—as pets! Are animals ever happy outside of the wild? Can wild beasts ever be tamed? (Scholastic 2005)

Before answering the textbook's summons to "turn the page and find out," let's try a little rewrite with a big word: ***love***.

> *Love* is at home in jungles, swamps, and open plains. But some *love* lives in zoos. Some even live(s) in people's homes—as pets! Is *love* ever happy outside of the wild? Can *love* ever be tamed?

Let's try it again with the word ***violence***. Logic forces us to make some additional copy changes.

> *Violence* is at home in jungles, swamps, and open plains. But some *violence* lives in zoos. Some even live(s) in people's homes—as *sibling rivalry*. Is violence ever *acceptable* outside of the wild? Can *violence* ever be tamed?

Discovering the power of figurative language in defining Big Words will enhance student writing across all disciplines. Using passages that you are reading in class for mentor text allows students to take a closer look at the content as well as the craft of the writer. Treating the new vocabulary word as a metaphor requires deeper thinking and the creation of connections at a profound level of understanding. Rarely will our hurdles in life be presented to us as a straightforward, multiple-choice question. Using this technique to define Big Words could prepare our students for also tackling big questions and then communicating their ideas to others.

"Language is man's way of communicating with his fellow man and it is language alone which separates him from lower animals," Maya Angelou tells us in the voice of Mrs. Flowers in *I Know Why the Caged Bird Sings*. "Words mean more than what is set down on paper. It takes the human voice to infuse them with shades of deeper meaning" (Angelou 1969). Anyone who has had the riveting pleasure of hearing Ms. Angelou speak understands that she knows how to give words additional meaning through her magnificent intonations. This is one reason why performance is such a crucial component in building word knowledge. If a student were to read a definition of ***tolerance*** with a note of sarcasm, for instance, perhaps incorporating "air quotes," the meaning of the writing could be changed entirely.

Let students know at the outset that they are writing for performance. This will motivate them to polish their writing and stimulate discussion as they prepare to write. We are providing three samples of mentor text that you may use to get started, and you can find projectable samples in Appendices W, X, and Y—but don't stop there!

> ***Sara:*** We didn't stop there. There's one of your poems in the box that follows.
>
> ***Michael:*** Yep. You can use that one, too. I used the warning labels off of the sides of a bottle of bleach, a can of insect repellant, and a can of paint thinner to compose it.

Figurative Language

Metaphorically Speaking

Mentor text can be as simple as the warning label on a can of spray paint, directions on a box of brownies, or the copy out of a catalogue—or it can come from a content-area textbook, poem, or piece of fiction. Since this venture into mentor text is also a lesson in figurative language, a higher-order thinking skill, our samples are arranged in progressive degrees of difficulty. You may choose one to fit the level of your classroom, or differentiate by discussing more than one sample. The first is very straightforward, a nonfiction sample taken from a National Geographic book: *Big Red Tomatoes* (Appendix W).

> Big, red tomatoes are smooth and round and juicy. Where do they come from? They are grown on farms. They are grown from seeds. Farmers put the tomato

911

hate is extremely flammable
its vapors may cause flash fire
hate is harmful if inhaled
keep hate away from heat, sparks,
and flame
do not breathe the vapors of hate
wash thoroughly after using hate
if you accidentally swallow hate
get medical attention

prejudice is an eye and skin irritant
its vapors too are harmful
do not get prejudice in eyes
or on clothing
prejudice is not recommended for use

(continues)

911 *(continued)*

by persons with heart conditions
if prejudice is swallowed induce
vomiting
if prejudice comes in contact with skin
remove clothing and wash skin
if breathing is affected, get fresh air
immediately

violence is harmful if absorbed
through the skin
keep violence out of the reach of
children
do not remain in enclosed areas
where violence is present
remove pets and birds from the
vicinity of violence
cover aquariums to protect from
violence
drift and run off from sites of violence
may be hazardous
this product is highly toxic
exposure to violence may cause
injury or death.

Michael Salinger (2007)

seeds into pots of soil. Soon, the seeds sprout . . . Water and sunshine help the plants grow. A tomato forms in the middle of the flower. At first the tomato is green. It grows bigger and bigger. Then, as it ripens, it turns red. (Graham 2001)

In our sample rewrite, we substituted *prejudice* for *tomatoes*—notice that *tomatoes* were plural, but in our rewrite, *prejudice* is singular. Rewrites often require a little grammatical tweaking to work; for example, ***wealth*** may turn into ***wealthy*** or ***tease*** into ***teasing***.

Sample Nonfiction Mentor Text for *Prejudice*

Prejudice is mean and closed-minded. It is grown around kitchen tables. It is grown from ignorance. Parents put *prejudice* into their kids' heads. Soon the *prejudice* sprouts. Hate and fear help *prejudice* grow. At first the *prejudice* is private. *Prejudice* grows bigger and bigger. Then as it ripens, it turns angry.

In our second sample, we have used one of Sara's poems, "Alone," rewritten with the word ***victory*** (Holbrook 2003). This one works particularly well because it closely aligns itself to the Collaboration Cheat Sheet, stating what the word doesn't have to be and can be. This simple format that will help students look at concrete possibilities to understanding abstract terms, such as *love, success, wealth* (see the Tier Two word list at the end of the chapter and Appendix X).

Our last piece of mentor text was written by poet Jimmy Santiago Baca. The definition is made more subtle by his initial statement that he doesn't know what ***racism*** is. As he proceeds to show the reader that

Alone

Alone
doesn't have to be sad
like a lost-in-the-city dog.

Alone
doesn't have to be scary
like a vampire swirled in fog.

Alone
can be slices of quiet,
salami in between
a month of pushy hallways
and nights too tired to dream.

Alone
doesn't have to be
a scrimmage game with grief.
Alone
doesn't have to argue,
make excuses or compete.
Like having nothing due,
sometimes.
Alone
is a relief.

Sara Holbrook (2003)

Victory

Victory
doesn't have to be loud
like a cannon erupting in the night.

Victory
needn't gloat
because it's won the fight.

Victory
can be proud
yet still be serene
offering a handshake
to the competing team.

Victory
doesn't have to be
all up in your face
Victory
Doesn't have to beat its chest
trash talk or belittle
to prove it is the best
sometimes
Victory
is grace.

Michael Salinger

he has intimate knowledge of *racism*, we are left to draw our own conclusions from his examples. By repeating his opening line as a conclusion, he twists his irony into the reader in a single stab. This sample (Appendix Y) was condensed from about a page and a half of writing in his book *C-Train and Thirteen Mexicans* (Baca 2002).

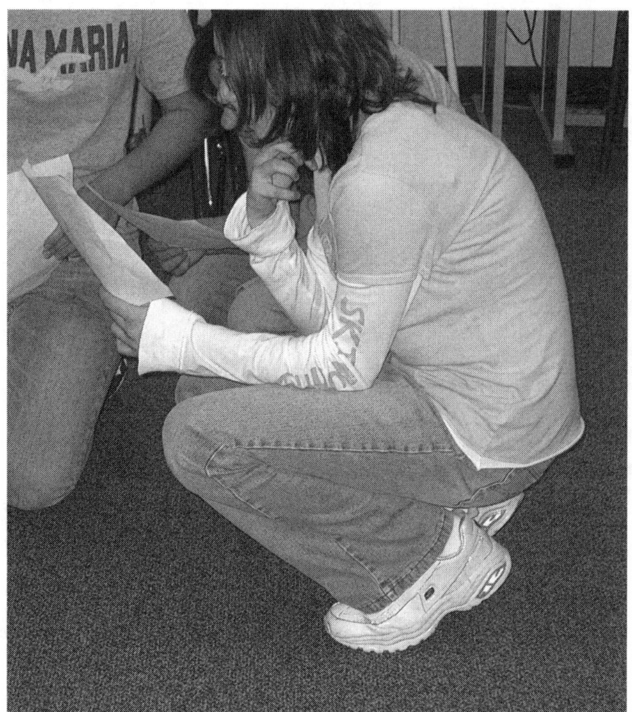

Figure 8.1 *Middle School Student Rehearses for Performance*

Sample Mentor Text for *Racism*

I deplore *racism*. I don't even know what the word means. I know what pain is, what death is, what a beating is at the hands of goon squads with lead-filled batons whacking bones, but the word *racism* is almost a joke these days . . . Millions of us survive in cardboard shacks in squalid camps without drinking water or even the most basic human facilities. No school. No medicine. We're paid a buck an hour. We're chased off the field before we get paid. We die from pesticide poisoning. We screech and gasp and die from sunstroke . . . I don't know what *racism* is. (Baca 2002)

Rewrite

I adore *peace*. I don't even know what the word means. I know what a smile is, what a warm sunspot is, what a laugh is on my grandmother's porch while we're sipping iced tea, but the word *peace* is just a Miss America joke these days . . . Millions of us survive in heated homes with plenty of fresh water and flush toilets. We grow up playing video games, hanging out with friends on the street, walking to the corner for a soda. No bombs dropping. No landmines. We're paid for our work. We're chased into safe beds at night. We live. We drum and sing along with the music on our iPods . . . I don't know what *peace* is.

Push the students to think of examples out of their own experiences. For instance, in the rewrite of Jimmy Santiago Baca's paragraph, the word *racism* has been changed to *peace*. As Baca has defined racism in terms he has personally seen, our rewrite does not describe the global kind of world peace that beauty pageant contestants talk about, but the kind of *peace* (and concrete examples) we can look for and find in our own lives.

Figure 8.2 *Sara leads sixth graders in a performance warm-up.*

Michael: A groovy kind of peace.

Sara: Isn't that a groovy kind of love?

Michael: According to poet Charles Bukowski, "Love Is a Dog from Hell."

Sara: The subject is *peace* and you are disturbing it, big-time.

The major pitfall to watch out for is the use of clichéd examples. Encourage the ideas to stretch their thinking by throwing them a couple curve balls during the group brainstorm and write. What does *family* sound like? Why? What does it not sound like? What does *racism* taste like? What does *friendship* smell like?

Figure 8.3 *Christine Landaker-Charbonneau confers with eighth-grade writers.*

Sara: One of my favorite examples came from a seventh grader in Old Greenwich, Connecticut, who suggested that *friendship* did not smell like cigarette smoke.

Michael: I like to push students one step further by adding connecting words, such as *because, although, but, like*, and *when*.

Sara: And you like this because . . .

Michael: Because I think it leads to deeper thinking about the word and promotes figurative language—oh wait, I get it.

A crucial component to encouraging students to think and write about Big Words is affording them an opportunity to say what they have learned aloud. Giving students an audience for their words and thoughts, guiding them toward active listening will go a long way toward building community and understanding in any classroom.

At first glance our list of suggested words may seem easy: *love, family, wealth*—these vocabulary words are right out of the primary grades. But a true understanding of what it really means to be *wealthy* is really a concept that of course changes as we mature.

Tier One: Basic Words

Easier	*Harder*
winner	champion
school	affluence
money	currency
gang	cult
popular	chic
family	kindred
club	alliance
relationship	rapport
conform	revolt
friendship	camaraderie
leader	commander
follower	disciple
bully	terrorist
suffering	anguish
tease	torment
pester	harass
effect	consequence
truth	reality
rumor	hearsay
negotiate	barter
conflict	quarrel
fight	brawl

Tier Two: Concept Words

Easier	Harder
love	adulation
hate	loathe
success	accomplishment
peace	harmony
prejudice	bigotry
wealth	affluence
fair	equitable
success	respect
war	conflict
lose	defeat
equality	parity
prosperity	opulence
happiness	bliss
justice	integrity
racism	intolerance
victory	triumph
beauty	exquisite
democracy	tyranny
cruelty	torture
revenge	vindictiveness
safety	security

Lesson Process

❶ **Share** the mentor text with students by projecting and reading aloud to the class. You may also want to provide copies of the text to the students since they will be basing their work on the original. Discuss the qualities of form (paragraph, essay, poem, etc.) and how the original author sought to define the word in terms of what it is and what it is not.

❷ **Choose and collaborate.** Pick a Big Word to work on with the class and complete a Collaboration Cheat Sheet for the word on the board as a group. This class discussion will help assign meaning to the term, deciding what the term is and is not. Point out that the words you will be working with in this exercise are not easily defined, but they are best described with concrete including sensory examples. Reinforce that in their rewrites, the students will not only change the word being defined, but they will come up with different concrete examples. This also gives you the opportunity to ask the students to assist in researching the word.

❸ **Group rewrite.** Rewrite the mentor text inserting the Big Word and soliciting help from the students, making any changes that enhance the quality or fluency of the piece. Leave this piece on the board as a reference for the students. Discuss how the Big Word colors the rest of the text around it now. Does the Big Word fit in this mentor text? Does the mentor text add any new insights to the meaning of the Big Word? This is also a good opportunity to bring up the concept of metaphor.

❹ **Provide time to read.** Pass out the mentor text(s) to the students. Give students time to read the text—especially if it is different from the one used in the modeling session. We have found students will be more engaged with the modeling session if they do not already have the mentor text in their hands vying for their attention.

❺ **Assign and collaborate.** Assign or have students select the Big Words. Encourage the kids to team up as they fill out their Collaboration Cheat Sheets even if they do decide to write on their own afterward.

❻ **Provide research material for the students.** Take a look back at our ideas about Researching Words in the Digital Age (page xi). Dictionaries and thesauruses can be augmented with essays and/or excerpts from longer texts about the Big Words they are writing about. A Google search for terms like *justice* and *essay* will return millions of hits.

❼ **Rewrite.** After kids complete their Collaboration Cheat Sheets, instruct them to rewrite their mentor texts using Big Words. Remind them that they may have to tweak their texts a bit to keep them within the realms of sense and fluency.

❽ **Turn and talk.** Students share their work out loud with someone near them. Allowing a bit of time for conversation between participants is a good idea as is walking around the room to be sure the conversations are pertinent to the lesson.

❾ **Perform.** Have student perform their works for the whole class. The type of mentor text being used will guide the type of performance.

❿ **Assess.** Lead the class in a discussion of the writing and performance they have just experienced. How does the Big Word set in the rewrite? Does this new angle add deeper understanding of the word? Is the rewrite successful in showing examples of what the word is and is not? Remember these are big concept words; we may never agree completely on their meaning but we can sure blaze some new synapse trails by thinking deeply about them.

⓫ **Hazards.** If students are having difficulty with this activity, try shortening the length of the copy they are to change. If they can't tackle a paragraph or an entire poem, have them just do one sentence or one verse.

> ***Michael:*** What about a haiku?
>
> ***Sara:*** Gesundheit.

The Collaboration Cheat Sheet

Word Conclusion

is / can / does	Version 1
an ending The caboose Closing arguments a buzzer ending The game end of The line in summary The last stop of The train tastes like dessert looks like a checkered flag	You can take it from here... Sara & Mo
is not / cannot / does not / won't not a starting gun a knock on The door doesn't sound like an overture. not The beginning not a drum major leading The band or The goose at The head of The V does not say, "curtain up"	

Conclusion

Appendix A

The Collaboration Cheat Sheet

Word ______________________________

	Version 1
is can does	
is not cannot does not won't	

Appendix B

Sample News Article for *Cataclysmic*

Riverside, OH—*Cataclysmic* ran through the front door Monday morning and straight into the trophy case at Riverside Middle School, scattering glass shards in the hallway and injuring fourteen students before tripping over his own feet and setting off the fire alarms causing the sprinkler system to go off and flooding the band room.

"I never saw such a messy, disastrous entry into the lobby," said Principal Ms. Sandra Smith. "*Cataclysmic* is a total wreck. We're very lucky there were no fatalities."

When asked to explain his behavior, *Cataclysmic* just shook his head and agreed that his actions were in fact dangerous. "Did you see all that broken glass?"

Principal Smith predicts that it will take days to restore order in the lobby and drain the band room and weeks to construct a new trophy case. Meantime, *Cataclysmic* will be serving detention for one month where he pledges that he will learn to become a productive student and how to enter the school without causing devastation, harming himself or others.

Appendix C

Sample Business Letter for *Inept*

Inept
333 Slippery Street
Unskilled, USA

Factory Founder
444 Efficient Row
Successful, USA
September 1, 2003 (or 2008, I can't remember)

Dear Mr. Founder:
I would like to apply for the job of manager of your manufacturing plant in Successful, USA. I am not the least bit qualified for this position because I am unskilled and clumsy. If you are looking for an employee you can really count on, that couldn't possibly be me.

I feel I have a lot to contribute to your organization. I know how to stall any project and can't problem solve at all. I am neither competent nor skilled in any way. I never do as I am told and rarely can handle any project sent my way.

If you are looking for someone you can count on to always drop the ball, I am your person.

Thank you for your kind attention. If you wish to contact me, look my number up yourself.

Sincerely,
Inept

Appendix D

Miscalculate Sequence Description

In order to *miscalculate*, follow this seven-step plan:

1. Pick ten apples.
2. Put them in a basket and count them again.
3. Make sure you have exactly a total of ten apples.
4. Pick two more apples.
5. Put those two apples in the basket and recount.
6. Add all the apples for a new total.
7. Announce that you now have fifteen apples in the basket.

Appendix E

Meander Sequence Description

In order to *meander*, follow this simple six-step plan:

1. Go to step three.
2. Wander aimlessly in and out of every room humming nonsensical tunes, then proceed to step four.
3. Go to step two.
4. Investigate any object at the edge of one's peripheral vision but not for any length of time that exceeds thirty seconds.
5. Do not move in a straight line under any circumstances; feel free to circle back.
6. Repeat step one.

Appendix F

Sample Obituary for *Insipid*

Topeka, Kansas (AP)—*Insipid*, a rather bland adjective, passed away on Monday of unknown causes. The age of the deceased was not readily recalled.

It is believed that *Insipid* may have died of boredom while painting his house beige. Passersby did not notice him until Thursday because he blended into his surroundings unremarkably.

Insipid's career as a doorstop spanned several decades yet none contacted could recall any achievements that could be credited to him. It seems *Insipid*'s life was marked by not standing out.

When asked to comment on *Insipid*'s life, surviving brother (and polar opposite), Spicy, replied, "I had a brother?"

Insipid is also survived by his wife, Boring; twin daughters, Tasteless and Soporific; and his son, Vapid.

In lieu of memorial services the family chose to watch grass grow.

Sample Obituary for *Convivial*

New Orleans, LA (*Party Time Magazine*)—*Convivial*, a very social adjective, died Saturday night surrounded by friends. *Convivial* passed away while dancing on a tabletop, wearing a lampshade on her head, and singing "Let's Get This Party Started."

Convivial's life was punctuated by one festive gathering after another. She was known as the life of the party, leading parades and making friends wherever she went. *Convivial* was elected the *most fun to be around* by her high school graduating class and lived up to that reputation.

Next-door neighbor Reticent said upon *Convivial*'s passing, "Finally we might get some peace and quiet in this building! Hopefully someone less social will move in now."

Memorial services for *Convivial* will be held in the grand ballroom of Caesar's Palace in Las Vegas starting on Thursday and are expected to continue for the next seven months.

Appendix H

Sample Interview for *Malevolent*

Malevolent applies for a position at a fast-food restaurant.

Q *What qualifies you for this position?*
A Well, first of all, I would have no problem selling unhealthy food to anyone. In fact, I would hope that anyone who came to the restaurant would end up sick. I could serve food past its expiration date without thinking twice—actually I would rather sell food that is rotten so I could help get rid of old inventory.

Q *What is your experience?*
A I really don't like people all that much so I think I would fit in well as counter help. I've become good at ignoring the needs of others by being mean to my little brother and I know I could carry this experience into my job here.

Q *What have you done to prepare you for this job?*
A I have served cereal to my little brother with spoiled milk and it didn't bother me at all when he blew chunks afterward. I even did it twice.

Q *What are your goals?*
A I just want to get my way—I really don't care if anyone gets hurt feelings because of my actions. Sometimes it's just more rewarding to see someone cry. I guess one of my goals is to make people feel really bad. I think I would find selling greasy food really rewarding.

Q *What are your strengths?*
A I don't let other people's feelings get in my way.

Q *What are your weaknesses?*
A I don't think I have any.

Appendix I

Sample Infomercial for *Enthusiasm*

Are you tired of being tired? Perplexed over being pooped? Fed up with fatigue?!

Hi!!! Millie Bays here and I want to introduce to you a brand-new product that will change your life—*ENTHUSIASM!* No more dragging your feet around the house or office annoying your friends, family, and coworkers. Just half a cup of *ENTHUSIASM* is all you need to turn the most mundane task into an enjoyable adventure because *ENTHUSIASM* is not just a product, *it's a way of life. ENTHUSIASM* gives you the get-up-and-go, sure, but that's not all. *ENTHUSIASM* includes the secret ingredient *INTEREST*, which keeps your energy and concentration at peak performance levels.

Watch as others around you become discouraged and give up, BUT NOT YOU! Because you had the keen insight to employ this amazing new product, *ENTHUSIASM!* Even the most common, humdrum tasks such as cleaning the cat's litter box, loading the dishwasher, or scrubbing the bathroom tiles become a pleasure when *ENTHUSIASM* is employed. ACT NOW and we will include *ENTHUSIASM*'s companion product, FERVOR, at absolutely no extra charge (you pay only for shipping and handling).

This is Millie Bays asking you to get yourself some *ENTHUSIASM!* (Product may not be effective in some institutions of higher learning or dentist's offices.)

Appendix J

Sample Op-Ed for *Exclusivity*

Open access to the library wastes money because it leads to the abuse of the books. Books are precious and they should not be allowed to circulate among the unwashed hands of mere students. Books need to be held for the *exclusive* benefit of teachers and librarians.

Restricted access to books will save money for the community. Worn books are worthless and allowing open library access wastes money and leads to tattered pages. Replacing lost or damaged books is very costly. When books are removed from the shelves, they must be put back, which increases work for librarians.

We must remove the word *public* from all libraries. Children particularly should be *excluded* from the library. They flip pages too fast and sometimes have food on their fingers. Last year students checked out books more than 800,000 times. Books were shared, toted in book bags, stashed in lockers, and taken home. This type of unrestricted use is dangerous for our books.

We must stop sharing books! Books should be for the *exclusive* use of teachers and librarians. Save money for our town and join me in restricting the free circulation of library books to just anyone.

Sincerely,
Exclusivity

Appendix K

Persuasive Oration for *Helium*

I am *Helium* and you should invite me to your party because I know how to keep things light. You may have heard that I do not play well with others. And that is true. I don't combine with my fellow chemicals at all. Instead I like to sneak around, odorless, colorless, some would say I am tasteless too, but I'm very entertaining. Most of those other chemicals smell like they never took a bath and they are simply TOO dense for me.

I hold myself apart, proud to be number two in the universe, knowing I am less dense than all the others (except for Hydrogen, who is so full of itself about being number one).

Don't hang with H! I never would.

I am popular, too! You should invite me to your party because I really know how to make balloons fly. We will go places in those balloons. We will! Even though it is my nature to be inert, I am NOT gravitationally bound. If you do not invite me to your party, you better watch it because WARNING! I have the lowest boiling point in the universe. So, invite me to your party today and for an added bonus, I'll make your voice go funny.

Appendix L

Sample Political Oratory for *Stealthily*

I, *Stealthily*, am your very best choice for dogcatcher. Vote for me on Tuesday. I have caught 99.9 percent of all animals I have set out to apprehend. Imagine that your new puppy is hiding under your porch but he is too scared to come out. I, *Stealthily*, have the ability to move without making a sound. I never crunch a twig under my feet or sneeze when I shouldn't. Unlike my clumsy opponent, *Ruckus*, who is noisy beyond compare, I am quiet as snow on the ground. I blend in with my surroundings when doing my job so I never get noticed, making me the perfect choice for the tricky position of dogcatcher. If I am elected dogcatcher all strays will be off the streets in less than a week and every new escaped dog will be caught within fifteen minutes because they will never see what got them! *Crafty*, the dogcatcher from one town over, says, "*Stealthily* is the sneakiest person I know." Vote for me if you want your loose dogs caught!

Appendix M

Sample Basic Nonfiction Narrative for *Carnivore*

Carnivore: Version 1

Fact: A true *carnivore* is an animal that eats only meat.

Fact: *Carnivores* either catch their food by hunting or they scavenge meat from already dead animals.

Unfortunately, *carnivores* are killers because they have short digestive systems that are not very good at breaking down plant material.

Fortunately, *carnivores* use their claws and sharp teeth to hunt and help strengthen their prey's population by mostly eating the weak or sick.

Finally, *carnivores* kill for food and will never become vegetarians.

Carnivore: Version 2

A *carnivore* is an animal that eats only meat, catching food by hunting or savaging.

They have short digestive systems, which don't break down plants well.

Using claws and sharp teeth, *carnivores* strengthen their prey's population by eating the weak and the sick.

Appendix N

Sample Basic Fictional Narrative for *Elation*

Elation: Version 1

Sentence 1: *Elation* was so happy it won the tournament that it screamed like a siren and jumped up straight in the air.

Sentence 2: Totally excited, it laughed and clapped and could not calm down.

Unfortunately, it couldn't act somber or get serious and got in trouble for making so much noise.

Fortunately, the outburst didn't last long and luckily, *Elation* avoided getting a penalty for showboating.

Finally, *Elation* skipped outside where it could really enjoy itself.

Elation: Version 2

Elation won the tournament! It screamed like a siren and jumped in the air, totally excited.

Elation couldn't calm down, act serious or somber.

No penalty for showboating, *Elation* skipped away.

Appendix O

Sample Diary Entry for *Nonconformist*

Today began with another bowl of Cheerios, just like yesterday and the day before. I boarded the bus at 7:30 A.M., right on schedule. All the rest of the kids on the bus were dressed identically—hooded sweatshirts and blue jeans, ragged at the edges and hanging down over their sneakers. Everything was the same.

Why does life have to be so monotonous? For instance, why can't some school buses in the United States be red or purple? Everywhere you go in this country the buses are yellow. Boring!

I crave something different. Life should be like a bouquet of wildflowers or at least a pile of multicolored gravel. Tomorrow I am not wearing the usual school uniform of jeans and a sweatshirt. I pledge to distinguish myself from everyone else. Tomorrow I will wear a prom dress to school or maybe a tuxedo. I will tie feathers to my ears and paint my face with glitter. Tomorrow I will just say *no* to conformity.

Signed,
Nonconformist

Appendix P

Character Description for *Flamboyant*

Flamboyant is a pink flamingo flapping in the lunchroom. She wears feathers in her hair and giant gold earrings. She is not shy and prefers singing to whispering. She wears rhinestones on her high-tops and purple eye shadow, and paints her nails lime green. *Flamboyant* is never mousy or plain. Instead she prefers to twirl through life, tap dancing to the tune of "If My Friends Could See Me Now."

Appendix Q

Sample Description of a Place for *Extravagant*

A visit to *Extravagant*'s crib reveals that he owns the most modern, most expensive condo on the Gold Coast. Behind the solid mahogany door is an entryway, which is floored in black marble. Overhead is a twirling mirrored ball reflecting 10,000 lights mounted in the ceiling and surrounding walls. His living room, kitchen, and bedroom glow in shades of gold, proving that he does not know the meaning of the word *economical*. His bathroom is bigger than the average living room. The sunken bath is topped with gold-plated fixtures sparkling in the sun pouring through the skylight. Standing like a throne against the back wall is a toilet with a heated seat with digital controls on the arm rests. Some might say that his crib is pretty gaudy, but one thing is for sure, *Extravagant* laid out some major cash to outfit his crib. He is definitely not cheap or stingy. *Extravagant*'s crib is just like he is, over the top.

Appendix R

Sample Description of a Thing for *Entanglement*

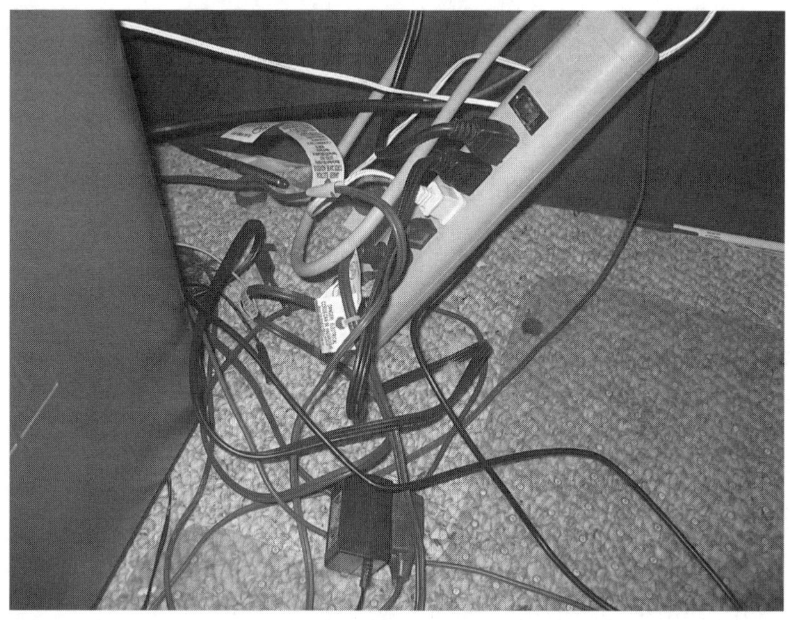

Beneath my desk, flanked by two lost pens, hangs an *entanglement* of wires. These brown and black wires make up the nerve center of my computer. The power strip dangles from the outlet, one end in the air and the other touching the beige carpet beside the grey computer. The wires twist and turn, braiding themselves into a mess that is almost impossible to sort or separate. Wires drop through a hole in the desk from different office machines (computer, printers, pencil sharpener, hard drive, phone, and lamp) and then snake into a ball of wires, an *entanglement* that is difficult to unravel.

Appendix S

Sample Definition Poem for *Subtle*

Subtle

Subtle
isn't a punch in the nose,
a kick in the shins,
a bee in the toes.

Subtle
stays quiet,
yet
everyone knows.

Sara Holbrook (1996)

Appendix T

Sample Definition Poem for *Redundant*

Redundant

Redundant.
Redundant.
Quit kicking my desk.
Redundant.
Redundant.
Please stop.
You're a pest.
Redundant.
Redundant.
You said that before.
Redundant.
Redundant.
Redundant.
NO MORE!
Sara Holbrook (2010)

Appendix U

Sample Definition Poem for *Novice*

Novice hasn't quite figured things out yet
you see he's just been sent into the game
doesn't have much experience
but he's more than willing to try just the same
it's not his fault, everyone has to start
somewhere at sometime
and I'm sure he's gonna
get the hang of things
I'm just saying . . . I'm glad he's your surgeon
and not mine.

Michael Salinger (2009)

Appendix V

Sample Definition Poem for *Reiterate*

Reiterate you can say that again!
and she will
sometimes re-phrased sometimes verbatim
but the message remains the same
for you see, *reiterate* conceives
that once is never enough
to get her message across
it's pretty tough competing
with all the noise of this busy world
so, she believes
a *notion* worth saying
is also worth repeating

Michael Salinger (2009)

Appendix W

Sample Nonfiction Mentor Text for *Prejudice*

Big, red tomatoes are smooth and round and juicy. Where do they come from? They are grown on farms. They are grown from seeds. Farmers put the tomato seeds into pots of soil. Soon, the seeds sprout . . . Water and sunshine help the plants grow. A tomato forms in the middle of the flower. At first the tomato is green. It grows bigger and bigger. Then, as it ripens, it turns red.

("Big Red Tomatoes" by Pamela Graham © 2001, National Geographic Society, Washington, DC)

Prejudice is mean and closed-minded. It is grown around kitchen tables. It is grown from ignorance. Parents put *prejudice* into their kids' heads. Soon the *prejudice* sprouts. Hate and fear help *prejudice* grow. At first the *prejudice* is private. *Prejudice* grows bigger and bigger. Then as it ripens, it turns angry.

Appendix X

Sample Mentor Text Poems

Alone

Alone
doesn't have to be sad
like a lost-in-the-city dog.

Alone
doesn't have to be scary
like a vampire swirled in fog.

Alone
can be slices of quiet,
salami in between
a month of pushy hallways
and nights too tired to dream.

Alone
doesn't have to be
a scrimmage game with grief.
Alone
doesn't have to argue,
make excuses or compete.
Like having nothing due,
sometimes.
Alone
is a relief.

Victory

Victory
doesn't have to be loud
like a cannon erupting in the night.

Victory
needn't gloat
because it's won the fight.

Victory
can be proud
yet still be serene
offering a handshake
to the competing team.

Victory
doesn't have to be
all up in your face
Victory
Doesn't have to beat its chest
trash talk or belittle
to prove it is the best
sometimes
Victory
is grace.

Appendix Y

Sample Mentor Text for *Racism*

"I deplore *racism*. I don't even know what the word means. I know what pain is, what death is, what a beating is at the hands of goon squads with lead-filled batons whacking bones, but the word *racism* is almost a joke these days . . . Millions of us survive in cardboard shacks in squalid camps without drinking water or even the most basic human facilities. No school. No medicine. We're paid a buck an hour. We're chased off the field before we get paid. We die from pesticide poisoning. We screech and gasp and die from sunstroke . . . I don't know what *racism* is."

Jimmy Santiago Baca

Rewrite: I adore *peace*. I don't even know what the word means. I know what a smile is, what a warm sunspot is, what a laugh is on my grandmother's porch while we're sipping iced tea, but the word *peace* is just a Miss America joke these days . . . Millions of us survive in heated homes with plenty of fresh water and flush toilets. We grow up playing video games, hanging out with friends on the street, walking to the corner for a soda. No bombs dropping. No landmines. We're paid for our work. We're chased into safe beds at night. We live. We drum and sing along with the music on our iPods . . . I don't know what *peace* is.

Works Cited

Allen, Janet. 1999. *Words, Words, Words: Teaching Vocabulary in Grades 4–12*. Portland, ME: Stenhouse.

Angelou, Maya. 1969. *I Know Why the Caged Bird Sings*. New York: Random House.

Baca, Jimmy Santiago. 2002. *C-Train and Thirteen Mexicans.* New York: Grove Press.

Beach, Richard, and Candance Doerr-Stevens. 2009. "Learning Argument Practices Through Online Role-Play: Toward a Rhetoric of Significance and Transformation," *Journal of Adolescent and Adult Literacy* 52 (6): 460–68.

Beck, Isabel, Margaret McKeown, and Linda Kucan. 2002. *Bringing Words to Life: Robust Vocabulary Instruction.* New York: Guilford Press.

———. 2008. *Creating Robust Vocabulary: Frequently Asked Questions and Extended Examples.* New York: Guilford Press.

Beck, Isabel L., Charles A. Perfetti, and Margaret G. McKeown. 1982. "Effects of Long-Term Vocabulary Instruction on Lexical Access and Reading Comprehension." *Journal of Educational Psychology* 74 (4): 506–21.

Beilock, Sian L. 2002. "Memory, Attention, and Choking Under Pressure." In *Sport and Exercise Psychology: International Perspectives*, edited by Tony Morris, Peter Terry, and Sandy Gordon. Morgantown, WV: Fitness Information Technology.

Berry, Wendell. 1983. *Standing by Words.* New York: Farrar, Straus.

Bradbury, Ray. 1990. *Zen in the Art of Writing.* New York: Joshua Odell Editions.

Cremation.com. 2009. "Planning for Cremation." www.cremation.com /index.php?option=com_content&Itemid=§ionid=16&id=117.

Daniels, Harvey, and Marilyn Bizar. 1998. *Methods That Matter: Six Structures for Best Practice Classrooms.* Portland, ME: Stenhouse.

Gallagher, Kelly. 2009. *Readicide: How Schools Are Killing Reading and What You Can Do About It.* Portland, ME: Stenhouse.

Graham, Pamela. 2001. *Big Red Tomatoes.* Washington, DC: National Geographic Society.

Graves, Donald. 1990. *Discover Your Own Literacy: The Reading/Writing Teacher's Companion.* Portsmouth, NH: Heinemann.

Griss, Susan. 1998. *Minds in Motion.* Portsmouth, NH: Heinemann.

Harvey, Stephanie, and Harvey Daniels. 2009. *Comprehension and Collaboration: Inquiry Circles in Action.* Portsmouth, NH: Heinemann.

Hinton, S. E. 1967. *The Outsiders.* New York: Viking Press.

Holbrook, Sara. 1996. *Am I Naturally This Crazy?* Honesdale, PA: Boyds Mills Press.

———. 1996. *The Dog Ate My Homework* Honesdale, PA: Boyds Mills Press.

———. 2002. *Wham! It's a Poetry Jam.* Honesdale, PA: Boyds Mills Press.

———. 2003. *By Definition: Poems of Feelings.* Honesdale, PA: Boyds Mills Press.

———. 2005. *Practical Poetry: A Non-Standard Approach to Meeting Content Standards.* Portsmouth, NH: Heinemann.

———. 2010. *Zombies! Evacuate the School.* Honesdales, PA: Boyds Mills Press.

Holbrook, Sara, and Michael Salinger. 2006. *Outspoken! How to Improve Writing and Speaking Skills Through Poetry Performance.* Portsmouth, NH: Heinemann.

Johnson, David W., and Roger T. Johnson. 2004. *Assessing Students in Groups: Promoting Group Responsibility and Individual Accountability.* Thousand Oaks, CA: Corwin Press.

Johnson, David W., Roger T. Johnson, and Edythe J. Holubec. 1993. *Cooperation in the Classroom.* 6th ed. Edina, MN: Interaction Book.

Johnson, Nancy. 2009. Email to Michael Salinger, 25 November.

Johnson, Thomas H. 1951. *The Complete Poems of Emily Dickinson.* Boston, MA: Little, Brown.

———. 1958. *Emily Dickinson, Selected Letters.* Cambridge, MA: Harvard College Press.

Keene, Ellin Oliver, and Susan Zimmermann. 2007. *Mosaic of Thought, Second Edition: The Power of Comprehension Strategy Instruction.* Portsmouth, NH: Heinemann

Li, May. 2008. "Ten Timeless Persuasive Writing Techniques." http://writing.learnhub.com/lesson/6026-ten-persuasive-writing-techniques.

McKeown, Margaret G., Isabel L. Beck, Richard C. Omanson, and Charles A. Perfetti. 1983. "The Effect of Long Term Vocabulary Instruction on Reading Comprehension." *Journal of Literacy Research* 15 (1): 3–18.

Molini, Sally, and Ted Kooser. 2009. "A Life in Poetry: Ted Kooser." *Cerise Press* 1 (1): 1–3. www.cerisepress.com/01/01/a-life-in-poetry-ted-kooser.

Nagy, W., P. Herman, and R. Anderson. 1985. "Learning Words from Context." *Reading Research Quarterly* 85 (Winter): 233–53.

Paz, Octavio. 1990. *The Monkey Grammarian.* New York: Arcade.

Salinger, Michael. 2007. *Stingray.* Ann Arbor, MI: Wordsmith Press.

———. 2009. *Well Defined: Vocabulary in Rhyme.* Honesdale, PA: Boyds Mills Press.

Sandburg, Carl. 2003. *The Complete Poems of Carl Sandburg, Revised and Expanded Edition.* New York: Houghton Mifflin Harcourt.

Schmidt, Eric. 2009. "Interview with Eric Schmidt," interview by Fareed Zakaria, GPS (CNN television), November 28, 2009. www.cnn.com/CNN/Programs/fareed.zakaria.gps/index.html.

Scholastic. 2005. *Read 180 R-Book.* New York: Scholastic.

Steineke, Nancy. 2009. *Assessment Live! 10 Real-Time Ways for Kids to Show What They Know—and Meet the Standards.* Portsmouth, NH: Heinemann.

Tatum, Alfred. 2005. *Teaching Reading to Black Adolescent Males.* Portland, ME: Stenhouse.

Whitaker, Sandra R. 2008. *Word Play: Building Vocabulary Across Texts and Disciplines Grades 6–12.* Portsmouth, NH: Heinemann.

Willems, Mo. 2003. *Don't Let the Pigeon Drive the Bus!* New York: Scholastic.

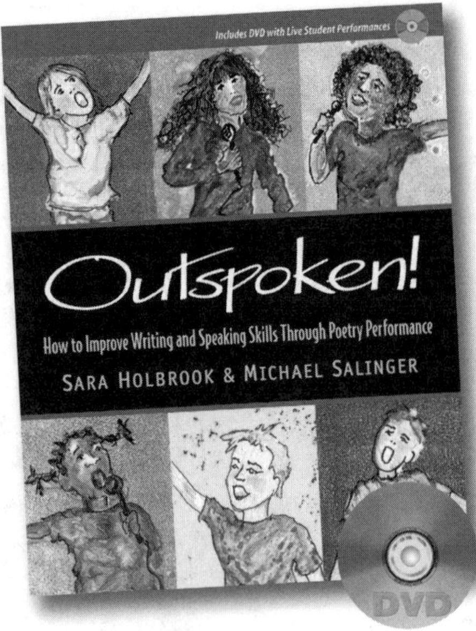
Includes DVD with Live Student Performances
Outspoken!
How to Improve Writing and Speaking Skills Through Poetry Performance
SARA HOLBROOK & MICHAEL SALINGER
DVD

Heinemann
DEDICATED TO TEACHERS